FAVORITE BIRDS
of the
SOUTHWEST

Text by
Dick Schinkel

Illustrations by
David Mohrhardt

With 125 Full-Color Illustrations

Thunder Bay Press

Favorite Birds of the Southwest ©1999 by Thunder Bay Press

Printed in China

03 02 01 00 99   5 4 3 2 1

ISBN 1-882376-46-3

Thunder Bay Press

P.O. Box 580 • Holt, Michigan 48842

Introduction

Arizona, California, Texas and other parts of the southwest are popular for vacations as well as retirement homes. Over the last few years, parts of Arizona and California have experienced tremendous population growth. Other than Florida, the southwest is as close to a tropical climate as we get. The southwest has the greatest diversity of habitats in the United States with mountains, rivers, shorelines, deserts, marshes, oceans, forests, grasslands, and agricultural areas. In addition, the southwestern states have a variety of preserved natural areas, parks, and national forests. The Pacific and Gulf coasts offer unprecedented birding opportunities as well as great pelagic birding.

During the winter, the southwest experiences a great influx of "snowbirds" from the north. Many people, retired or otherwise, spend a great deal of their winter months there to avoid the frigid and stormy north. Many resort, tour agencies, hotels, and communities now actively cater to the birding population. Many local chambers of commerce have put together festivals to celebrate times of the year or certain birds. Two of the most popular are the Whooping Crane and Hummingbirds. Nowhere in the United States can one see the Whooping Crane with such ease. During the season, you may be able to see more than a dozen species of hummingbirds, many other species found in North America, and some rarities.

Probably more books exist about birding in the southwest than any other part of the United States. In the past, birdwatching was considered an oddity. Today it is the rule and heavy competition exists to attract this part of the tourist trade. Texas and Arizona are probably the most popular states in the southwest for birders. These states border Mexico and offer a variety of birds found nowhere else. After the summer rains, many tropical birds move northward from Mexico to escape the heat and some summer birds take up residence and are increasing in population. Migration time is also a popular time to see birds as the bulk of passerine birds move up from Central and South American through these states. Many birds also winter in the southwest because of the mild climate and diverse habitat.

The intent of this book is to provide a reference for the beginner as well as for the enthusiast who has an agenda for specific birds. This book will not attempt to cover all four hundred plus species of birds that can be found in the southwest, but features those that most often attract the attention of the beginning birder and that can be found easily in the most visited places in the southwest. In many cases, plumages of different seasons are given or described because plumages will usually be represented at one or more times of the year. The topography of a bird is given to help in field identification.

The birds discussed in this text are fairly easily found in the correct habitat at the proper time of the year. It is recommended that a diary be kept in this book by writing where and when you first sighted a bird on the page that the bird is listed. A few notes will help you to recall what was seen and aid in recalling places and events. Keeping this diary is very rewarding and is similar to keeping a family album. Indeed, these birds will become part of your family.

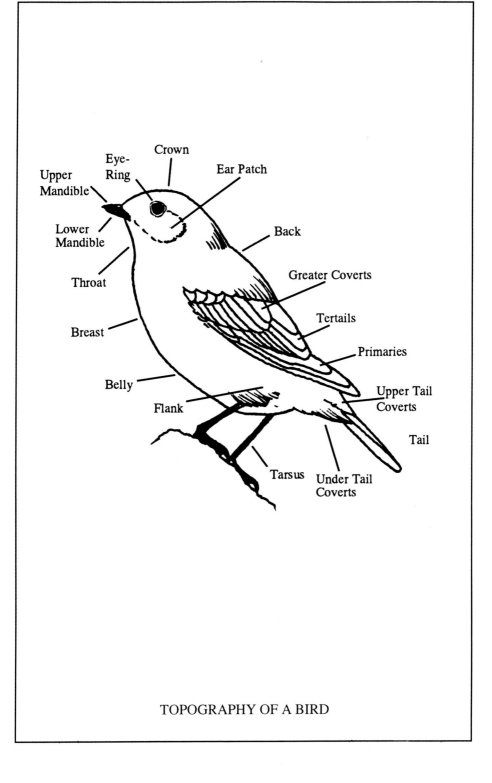

TOPOGRAPHY OF A BIRD

COMMON LOON *Gavia immer*

In England this bird is called a 'Diver' and it sure lives up to its name, diving deep into the water to catch fish with its long dagger-like bill. It catches fish of all sorts up to nearly a foot in length. The Common Loon dives underwater and swims after the fish with its powerful feet. It is opportunistic in feeding and will take anything that it can catch and eat. They have been known to take leeches, frogs, large insects, and tadpoles.

The Loon can be as long as three feet and is quite sleek with its black head and black-checkered body. Its neck has a necklace of white markings from the back which fade away, picking up again just under the chin. The Indians think this necklace is sacred and used the feathers in headdresses and ceremonial garments. Its eye is quite red in breeding birds and its bill is stout and pointed. Winter birds most commonly seen along the coast and Gulf of Mexico are dull-gray in color with a light-gray neck with uneven markings, making it easy to distinguish the Common Loon from the winter Arctic Loon which has a clear demarcation of the dark and gray neck patch. The winter Red-throated Loon is smaller with a very slim bill and almost all gray-white neck.

In flight, the Loon carries its head and neck down and its feet hang behind the short tail, giving it an awkward look. During migration the Loon may be found on larger inland lakes but it is most common during the winter in the Pacific Ocean and the Gulf of Mexico. The call of the Loon is a series of wails and yodels. Unfortunately, during the non-breeding season calls are extremely rare and it is very uncommon to hear them in the southwestern United States. The Common Loon breeds almost exclusively in Canada, Alaska, and a few northern states such as Minnesota, Wisconsin, Michigan, New York, and Maine in the east and a small part of Washington and Idaho in the west.

In nesting, sibling rivalry sometimes exists and the first hatchling may attempt to eliminate the second chick. The two olive-spotted eggs are laid in a nest extremely close to shore as the Loon is not able to travel comfortably over land. Both sexes incubate the eggs for an average of twenty-eight days. The young stay with the adults until fall and learn to swim and dive in one day. The young ride on the adults' back as they are growing and are extremely well protected by both parents. With more emphasis on the protection of this magnificent bird it is making a comeback from previous population losses.

Common Loon

PIED-BILLED GREBE *Podilymbus podiceps*

Although the Pied-billed Grebe breeds over the southwest it is most common during the winter when the state is inundated with migrants. During the winter it is brown overall with a yellow bill, yellow eye-ring and whitish chin and throat. This bird can be seen in almost any body of water whether it be fresh, salt or brackish. It will float along and dive for fish and small crustaceans or may just submerge itself from a full floating position or to any stage of submerged body.

During the breeding season its bill is white with a black band around it and a black chin and the throat is evident. The eye-ring is white and its light-brown body is a darker brown. A shallow floating platform of vegetation is used as a nest. It is anchored among rushes or reeds in open water for protection. The outer part of the nest may contain a ring of green duckweed, algae, or pond weeds that the bird can reach while incubating the eggs.

The four or five eggs hatch in a little over three weeks. The chicks are quite striking, with pronounced streaking, appearing almost zebra-like with black-and-white stripes. After a short time (usually a day) the chicks are able to follow the parents and will ride upon the parents' backs. After a month or so the chicks will go through rapid growth and change and soon will be able to leave the parents, although they will remain together as a family group for a while longer. Nesting can occur from early March through late fall, although most nesting is usually complete by September.

During the non-breeding season the Pied-billed Grebe is mostly solitary but occasionally it can be found feeding in open water in small loose groups. A very poor flier, the Grebe will dive to hide itself and appear with only its head above water to assess the situation. It can swim a great distance under water to escape predation. If you are near the Pied-billed Grebe in the water it will not appear overly concerned but each time it dives it appears just a little further away from you than when it submerged.

The calls of this small bird are not characteristic of its size but more characteristic of marsh birds who must be loud to be heard. The call is similar to that of the Cuckoos. The call starts rather fast and slows down as it finishes its song. The call starts with the *coo coo coo* and then goes into a *cow cow cow* finishing to a slower paced *kup kup kup kup*. This call can be heard in breeding season at any time of day or night.

4

Pied-billed Grebe

HORNED GREBE AND EARED GREBE

Podiceps auritus / Podiceps nigricollis

These two grebes are similar in size and shape but differ in coloration, breeding range, and wintering populations in the southwest. This bird is a diver much like the Common Loon and uses its sharp beak to capture aquatic organisms. The Grebe's silhouette is similar to that of the Loon but its bill, although just as pointed, isn't as massive. In breeding plumage, both Grebes have bright golden tufts on the side of the head—hence the names 'eared' or 'horned.' The Eared Grebe generally has the more impressive tufts. The main difference in these two Grebes are their necks.

In breeding plumage the Horned Grebe is a dark-cinnamon color where the Eared Grebe is black. Both birds have red eyes. More commonly seen in the winter, it is most important to be able to distinguish between the two in winter plumage. Instead of the black and cinnamon colors, the Grebe's winter plumage becomes gray and white. To identify them we must look at their necks and heads. The Horned Grebe has distinct demarcations with a white neck and lower half of its head. The top of its head is black. The neck of the Eared Grebe is gray, graduating to white in its throat and to a prominent white patch behind its eye that goes above the eye line.

In the southwest, these birds are found mostly along both coasts but the more common Eared Grebe can be found throughout the entire southwest anywhere there is water, especially in winter. The Eared Grebe does breed in parts of the southwest but is not regular. The breeding area of the Eared Grebe is the western states where there are prairie potholes and small lakes and marshes. The breeding territory extends into Canada but stops about the eastern edge of the Dakotas. The Horned Grebe breeds in the same habitat except it is found further north into Canada and Alaska. Only in the northern parts of Idaho, Montana, and the Dakotas north does this bird nest in the United States.

The Horned Grebe seems to prefer marshes over ponds and the more open waters that the Eared Grebe prefers. Both Grebes build their nests in shallow water, constructing them from floating mats of pond vegetation interwoven with existing standing vegetation. Usually four or five eggs are laid and incubated by both parents for about three weeks. The young are able to follow the parents after a day and like the Loon they ride upon the parents' back. Normally one brood is hatched yearly.

The Grebes eat insects, small fish, crustaceans, tadpoles or anything which presents itself. Summer food is predominately insects with an increase in fish during the winter. Populations are stable to declining, primarily due to human pressure on the wintering grounds. More at risk is the Eared Grebe because it overwinters on smaller inland waters than the Horned Grebe.

6

Top: Horned Grebe (Winter Head)
Below: Eared Grebe (Winter Head)

BROWN AND AMERICAN WHITE PELICAN
Pelecanus occidentalis / Pelecanus erythrorhynchos

Every school child knows the large bird with the pouch, the Pelican. In the southwest two species of Pelican are present, the American White Pelican and the Brown Pelican. With a wingspan reaching nearly ten feet the Pelican is an impressive bird, and is common on the coasts and waterways of the southwest. Unlike egrets, these large white birds have black wing tips when flying.

The White Pelican is abundant during the winter months as a winter resident while the Brown Pelican breeds in the southwest. The Brown Pelican is more common along the coastline but occasionally can be found on inland lakes and waterways. The American White Pelican breeds in the middle of the North American continent into the prairies of Canada and winters on the coasts of Florida. In a few small isolated areas the White Pelican is a summer breeder.

When feeding the White Pelicans swim along, usually in groups, thrusting their heads simultaneously into colonies of small fish, filling their pouch with water and fish. After pulling their heads above water, the water escapes from the pouch through a narrow slit between the two bills, trapping the fish inside. The bill is then tilted upward and the fish swallowed.

The Brown Pelican feeds entirely differently. It dives into the water from the air, engulfing fish with its large bill and pouch. It then bobs to the surface and allows the water to drain from its down-turned bill until it can raise its head and swallow the captive fish. The Brown Pelican feeds solitarily or in small loose groups. The Brown Pelican is not particularly afraid of man so it is found feeding from docks and piers along many waterways, especially where fishermen discard fish entrails. If you happen to find an area where the pelican is diving and you can snorkel, it is quite a sight to see them plunge into the water just ahead of you. Snorkelers may actually encourage the pelicans by disturbing schools of fish for them to feed upon.

Brown Pelicans usually lay two to three white eggs. They build a nest in trees or mangroves but may nest on the ground as the American White Pelican does. The eggs will hatch in four to five weeks, with the White Pelican taking longer. The time from hatching to leaving the nest varies on the food supply but usually it is several months.

When DDT was in use the Brown Pelican was in extreme danger of extinction. The DDT caused the eggshells to become soft and break in the nest before hatching. When DDT was declared illegal, Florida held the only hope for the Brown Pelican. The population has come back in grand form, although habitat loss is still a concern.

8

Brown Pelican and American Pelican

DOUBLE-CRESTED CORMORANT

Phalacrocorax auritus

The Double-crested Cormorant is named for the two plumes or crests that arise from its eye-line during the breeding season. Many people who have never had a close look at this bird during the breeding season think that the double crest comes from the flight silhouette the neck gives to the head. It appears that the head has a slight crest coming from the back much like that of a Cardinal.

The Double-crested Cormorant is black all over and stands about three feet tall. Adult birds have orange throat pouches during the entire year. Immature birds have light-colored throats and chests. The bill of the Cormorant is hooked at the end to catch fish. The Cormorant flies with its neck outstretched with a little bend, whereas the Common Loon, which sometimes can be confused with the Cormorant, flies with its head below the body.

The Double-crested Cormorant is common on the coastline where it feeds on fish. It can be found resting on piers, shrubs, rocks, and buildings. It can be seen drying its outstretched wings after swimming for fish. This is similar to the Anhinga except the Cormorant is entirely black where the Anhinga has white shoulders. Populations are on the increase in the southwest as well as throughout many parts of the United States, especially in the interior. During the winter, the population is increased by the influx of northern migrants. While in migration the Cormorant will fly in a 'V' formation much like Canada Geese.

The nesting of Cormorants occurs mainly in colonies with herons and storks. Their nests are built in trees and mangroves. Three or four bluish-tinted eggs are laid in the nests and are incubated for about four weeks. They take another five to six weeks to fledge. The young need brooding for about two weeks before being left alone while the parents feed. The young are fed regurgitated fish: first nearly digested liquid, later fish pieces, and finally whole small fish.

The Double-crested Cormorant is very successful at diving to catch fish. You may see them swimming along with just their head above water slowly sinking from sight. In some freshwater areas the increase of Cormorants has caused concern over the decrease in fish populations.

As in many of the birds that are dependent on fish for a living, the Cormorant populations were hurt dramatically when DDT was in unsupervised use. With the ban on DDT, hard pesticides, and unnatural chemicals the waters of the lakes and oceans have seen a remarkable population comeback occur especially in the interior of the United States.

Double-crested Cormorant

ANHINGA *Anhinga anhinga*

The Anhinga, or Water Turkey as it is sometimes called, can be found throughout the eastern half of Texas, especially inland on fresh and brackish waters. Winter migrants add to the small breeding summer populations present in Texas.

The male is black overall except for its white shoulders and upper wings. The female has a buff-brown neck instead of black. The Anhinga is similar to the Cormorant in shape and size. Major differences are in the sharp-pointed bill of the Anhinga as opposed to the hooked bill of the Cormorant. The Anhinga has a longer and much slimmer neck than the Cormorant and its tail is much longer. The feathers of the Anhinga are not as waterproof, which allows it to be able to dive and swim after fish with relative ease. Because its feathers get quite wet, the most common pose you will see is the Anhinga with its wings spread and drying.

The Anhinga feeds on aquatic animals, impaling them with its sharp bill, bringing them to the surface, flipping the prey into the air and swallowing it. Fish and larger prey are usually swallowed head first. The Anhinga, like the Loon and the Cormorant, can submerge itself and swim around with only its head and neck above water, giving it the name of "Snake Bird."

A nest of loose sticks is built by both sexes, usually in low shrubs or trees such as mangrove and willows, like those of herons, ibis, and egrets. Three to six bluish-white eggs are laid in the nest and tended by both sexes. Four weeks of incubation are required to hatch the eggs. The time for fledging is variable, depending upon the food supply and number of chicks in the nest, but can last for four to six weeks. As the young near fledging, they will begin to move around with the aid of their feet, wings, and bill. Nesting usually begins during March and will continue through June.

The Anhinga is the perfect symbol of the southwest's freshwater areas. In some parts of the world, the Anhinga is harnessed to capture fish. A ring is placed around the neck to prevent the Anhinga from swallowing the fish, thereby providing food for its owner.

Anhinga

GREAT BLUE HERON *Ardea herodias*

The Great Blue Heron can be found in wet areas along roadside ditches, lakes, streams, estuaries, and coastal shorelines. The Great Blue Heron, Great Egret, and Cattle Egret are the most common large wading birds found in the southwest. The Cattle Egret and Great Egret are white, whereas the Great Blue Heron is gray-blue. The Great Blue Heron stands around four feet in height with a wing-span of five to six feet.

The Great Blue Heron feeds upon any aquatic creature that it can catch while wading in shallow water but it prefers fish as its staple food. Due to its close proximity to man, the Heron has become quite adaptable to other food sources. At camp sites Herons take mice as well as a full-grown gray squirrels.

The Great Blue Heron is colonial in nesting, preferring to situate its nest in "rookeries" containing a few dozen to several hundred nests. Most often the same nesting areas are used year after year. The nests are loosely con-structed of sticks and leaves. They can be from ten to over fifty feet from the ground, the height depending on the vegetation available. In the south where tall trees are at a premium, nest-ing occurs in mangroves and willows. Three to four light blue-green eggs are laid in the nest beginning in Novem-ber. Four weeks are needed to hatch, with six to eight weeks to fledging, again dependent upon the food sup-ply. Both parents incubate and feed the chicks. Predation of young is great while on the nests.

In the southwest, a white phase (White Morph) of the Great Blue Heron is found. This bird has a com-pletely white body with yellow legs and yellow bill. "Wurdemann's Heron" is supposed to be an interme-diate bird between the two herons or possibly an offspring of mixed mat-ing.

The Great Blue Heron is a great study in patience and stalking. Be-cause its legs are quite long, the Blue Heron can wade and feed in relatively deep water. Sometimes it will wait in water up to its lower body waiting for a fish or tadpole to swim by. If the fish is small it is usually swallowed on the spot, but occasionally the Heron will take a larger fish or snake to the shore where it will drop it and strike it repeatedly before swallowing it whole. As long as there is some suc-cess in capturing food the Heron will return to feed. This has caused major consternation with fish farms as well as to the backyard pond enthusiast. The legal and most expedient way to stop the Herons from feeding is to place a network of lines, netting, or some sort of protection over the pond.

Great Blue Heron

GREAT EGRET *Casmerodius albus*

The Great Egret and the Cattle Egret are probably the most recognizable of the birds that visitors see on the ditches and lakes of the southwest. Similar in size to the Great Blue Heron, the Great Egret is completely white with a yellow bill which changes to bright-orange during breeding season. It has black legs and feet. Although the Great Egret is found quite extensively to the north, it is truly a southern bird, being quite common except in the deserts and mountains. During the winter an influx of northern migrants come into the southwest.

Nesting occurs during the winter months, three eggs normally being laid. The nests are loose platforms of sticks and twigs with finer material lining the center. They are built in trees and shrubs from ten to fifty feet above the ground. The nests in the colonies sometimes number in the hundreds and they are often found mixed together with those of other wading birds. Most nests are built from ten to thirty feet apart.

The light-blue eggs take nearly four weeks to hatch and the young are fed regurgitated soft food at first, but soon begin to eat food left behind by the parents. The young are able to leave the nest at about four weeks. One brood of young is raised each year and the success of nesting is increasing with the ban of DDT and more environmental awareness. However, the Great Egret still has to com-pete with the loss of its wetland habitat.

Historically, the Great Egret, as well as some of the other egrets, were slaughtered for their beautiful breeding plumes. If you see these birds displaying during the breeding season you will understand the attraction for their exotic and exquisite plumes. Not much thought was given to the effect of collecting the birds' feathers during the mid-1800s. It wasn't until the turn of the century that laws were passed and the use of plumes and feathers was no longer acceptable. Now it is a conservation symbol of the Audubon Society.

The Great Egret is a little more aggressive in its feeding habits than the Great Blue Heron. It will remain still and wait for its prey to swim or hop by, but it is also an aggressive stalker. Many times it will sneak up on a fish, frog, or other aquatic prey and capture it in its long pointed bill. Occasionally it will feed with other wading birds and even steal from nearby ibis, storks, and herons.

Great Egret

CATTLE EGRET *Bubulcus ibis*

This prolific and abundant white wading bird has an interesting history. The Cattle Egret is an import from Africa. The first Cattle Egret showed up in South America in the late 1800s and arrived in Florida and Texas by the middle of this century. The first breeding record occurred in the early 1950s. They have since expanded throughout the southern states. The migratory and wandering habits of this bird cause it to show up in nearly every state east of the Mississippi. It has reached the west coast and is moving north from California.

In Africa, the Cattle Egret is known for following antelopes and other grazers of the savanna. As the land in Africa was taken over by farms and cattle, this bird began following cattle, hence the name Cattle Egret. The Cattle Egret is also known to sit on the backs of large animals such as the cape buffalo, elephant, and rhinoceros. In the United States it is known to ride on the backs of livestock and even alligators. In agricultural areas, the Cattle Egret has even adapted to following tractors tilling the soil searching for anything edible that might appear, from worms to mice.

This small egret is very common throughout the southwest, especially during the breeding season. During the winter, the Cattle Egret flies even further south so it is less abundant throughout the area.

The breeding season is from March through the summer. Except during the breeding season, this small egret (eighteen to twenty inches) is all white with a yellow bill and yellowish-colored legs. In the breeding season the bird has rusty plumes on its head, back, and lower neck. During breeding its legs become darker and its bill becomes bright-orange. This egret is a little more stocky and has shorter legs than other egrets. There is no place that this bird cannot be found except in deeply-forested areas.

The Cattle Egret prefers to hunt in open areas, both dry and wet, where it seeks insects, small birds, mice, reptiles, and amphibians. It normally takes advantage of other animals or humans to flush its prey.

The loose nest of reeds, sticks, and twigs is placed in tall shrubs or small trees. Usually three or four light-blue eggs are laid in the nest and incubated by both sexes for just under four weeks. One adult broods the young for about three weeks. The young can leave the nest and be self-sufficient after a few more weeks.

The Cattle Egret has become a suburban bird in some instances. An opportunist, the Cattle Egret will raid gardens and even dog bowls, although this behavior is not common enough to become a nuisance, probably because of the preference for a diet of living things.

Cattle Egret

SNOWY EGRET *Egretta thula*

This middle-sized Egret is most easily distinguished from the other egrets by its bright-yellow feet and black bill. The Snowy Egret's upper legs are black, which accentuates the black slipper-look of its feet. Its bill has a yellow spot in front of its eye which turns bright-orange during the breeding season.

Another characteristic of the Snowy Egret which distinguishes it from other egrets is its active style of feeding. It rushes about seeking fish, frogs, and other aquatic life. It is different from the white phase of the Reddish Egret, not only because it has yellow feet and a straight black bill but because the Reddish Egret is usually a bit larger and spreads its wings when feeding. The immature white phase of the Little Blue Heron has yellow legs and a gray- to flesh-colored bill.

Like the other egrets, the Snowy Egret was hunted to near extinction for its plumes. The Snowy Egret has rebounded nicely, although in recent years their numbers seem to be declining. It is found throughout the southwest but can be common in one area and almost absent in others. In the southwest, the Snowy Egret summers in northern California and the 'quad' states and winters along the coastlines as well as being a permanent resident in these areas.

The normal nesting season is from March through early summer but occasionally it may begin a little earlier.

Nesting in colonies with other egrets and herons, the Snowy Egret places its nest of loosely-stacked sticks in trees and shrubs about ten to thirty feet above the ground. The male gathers the nesting material and the female builds the nest.

The three to five eggs take about three weeks to hatch and the hatching is staggered over several days. Because of this staggered hatching, the youngest chicks may not survive during years of lean food supplies. The young are able to leave the nest about four weeks after hatching. Only one brood is produced each year.

During breeding, the Snowy Egret sports beautiful plumes of feathers like the Great Egret. The Snowy Egret is a much more striking bird during breeding season because of its jet-black legs and striking yellow feet. As in most of the egrets, its bill color changes dramatically during breeding.

The Snowy Egret also has the habit of following some of the more active wading birds, such as the Glossy Ibis and Reddish Egret, in order to take advantage of their active feeding and to capture food stirred up by these birds.

Snowy Egret

GREEN-BACKED HERON *Butorides striatus*

This small heron is eighteen inches tall, and is one of the most secretive. Preferring to remain hidden, the Green-backed Heron habituates wooded swamplands throughout extreme southern Texas. Not as colonial as some of the other herons, the Green-backed Heron (formerly called the "Green Heron") normally feeds solitarily.

The Green-backed Heron is a small chubby bird with an iridescent green back. Its legs are yellow-green; the male's legs become bright-orange during breeding season. Its cape, or neck, is russet-colored with a white stripe running down the neck, similar to the Tricolored Heron.

The Green-backed Heron is the most solitary and sedate of the herons in feeding, infrequently pursuing its prey. Its usual method of obtaining food is to sit on a log, branch, or along the bank waiting for a fish, frog, or some small crustacean to happen along. It may remain motionless for long periods of time while waiting for just the correct moment. When the fish is within striking distance the heron will lash out its long neck and pierce the fish with its bill. If the fish is small it will flip it up into the air and swallow it headfirst. If the fish is large, it may wade ashore and position it in order to swallow it. The larger bill of this heron allows it to catch larger prey.

Nesting begins in March and is completed by June. Usually, the Green-backed Heron is a solitary nester in trees and shrubs of about thirty feet. In suburban areas, it likes to nest in clumps of coniferous trees. Occasionally it will nest with others of its species; even more rarely it nests with other herons, ibis, or egrets. A platform of intertwined twigs and sticks is created and holds about four bluish-green eggs. Often the nest will be near, even overhanging, the water.

The eggs hatch in about three-and-one-half weeks and the young will leave in another four weeks. Before leaving the nest the young climb about the nest and tree with ease. The young cannot take care of themselves for another month and are attended to by the adults until the youngsters learn to forage for themselves.

Green-backed Heron

REDDISH EGRET *Egretta rufescens*

The Reddish Egret is found along the Gulf of Mexico in Texas and straying up from Baja California to extreme southern California. Although not as common as the other egrets and wading birds, the population has made enough of a comeback from the plume hunters to become common again. The best sites to view these birds is in the refuges along the coast of Texas. During the non-breeding season, this bird can be found in wet areas in Florida, Alabama, Georgia, Louisiana, and Texas.

Breeding may begin as early as December but normally begins in early spring and proceeds through late spring. Breeding plumes are present during the season along with blue patches in front of its eyes. Its bill is flesh-colored with a black tip. Both sexes build a platform of twigs in small shrubs and trees as well as mangroves.

Three or four light-blue eggs are laid and hatch in about four weeks. The young are fed regurgitated food; as they become older the pieces of food become larger. The young can leave the nest at about five weeks but will still be dependent upon the parents for as long as five more weeks.

The Reddish Egret gets its name from the reddish "mane" the bird exhibits. Its body is gray. Its legs are blue-black in color. A white phase of the Reddish Egret is easily distinguished from the other white egrets by its leg and bill color. The Reddish Egret is about thirty inches tall, making it medium in size among the egrets and herons.

Besides its color, the feeding habits of the Reddish Egret most distinguish it from other egrets. The Reddish Egret is one of the most aggressive wading birds. It spreads its wings and dashes back and forth pursuing fish and aquatic invertebrates. In a flock of birds feeding in the shallows of an estuary or lake edge, it is easy to pick out the Reddish Egret by its fits and starts as it darts to and fro chasing fish.

Some feel the Reddish Egret's spread wings give it the advantage of seeing its prey by cutting down glare from the sun while others propose that the shadow of the egret lures fish to a hiding place. The Reddish Egret may also be stirring up the bottom to chase out hidden prey. This egret is not adverse to taking advantage of prey stirred up by other wading birds, so you may find the Reddish Egret feeding among flocks of ibis, storks, and other herons and egrets.

Reddish Egret

TRICOLORD HERON   *Egretta tricolor*

The Tricolored Heron was originally called the "Louisiana Heron." This medium-sized heron is just over two feet tall. The Tricolored Heron is easily distinguished from the other bluish-colored herons because of its size, blue head, and zipper-like white stripe down the front of its neck. It has a white belly, while the Little Blue Heron is entirely blue. The Great Blue Heron has white on its head and a light-gray neck instead of blue. The Tricolored Heron has a yellow bill with black tip whereas the Little Blue Heron's bill is black or bluish. Although not extremely common, this bird can be found nearly anywhere in the eastern half of Texas in shallow wetland areas.

During the winter, local populations may be increased by migrants. Even though this bird was not as heavily sought after for its plumes the population is still not large today. As in all wetland-dependent animals, the populations are being reduced by the loss of wetland habitats. The Tricolored Heron can be found along the Gulf coast and to the Carolinas on the Atlantic coast.

As with all egrets and herons, the Tricolored Heron feeds on fish, frogs, aquatic invertebrates and anything else it can catch. This heron is good at stalking and may be aggressive in chasing schools of fish or tadpoles. You may see this heron walking across mats of water lettuce or water hyacinths as it searches for insects, frogs, and crayfish.

A nest of loosely-arranged sticks is placed in shrubs and mangroves. Nesting begins in February and the nests are abandoned by spring. The nest is built by both parents and the three to four blue-green eggs are incubated by both parents for just over three weeks. The young are tended by both parents as well. As with most herons, the young are fed well-digested regurgitated food at first. As the chicks get older, they begin to eat small pieces of fish until they can swallow small fish and insects whole.

The young are mature enough to leave the nest and fend for themselves at about five weeks. The immature birds have a russet-brown wash over the back and rump. The nests are usually found in colonies with the nests of other herons, egrets, and ibis. Most often the nests are near saltwater and they do not occur with any regularity in the interior.

Immature birds and migrating birds can become quite the wanderers north of their normal coastal range, however their affinity for saltwater probably limits their populations to the coastlines of the United States. As in many parts of Florida the elimination of wetlands will be a dramatic factor in population numbers and growth.

Tricolored Heron

WHITE IBIS   *Eudocimus albus*

Although many do not realize it, this white wading bird is probably one of the most numerous of the ibis in coastal Texas with the possible exception of the Cattle Egret. The White Ibis may be found throughout eastern Texas in marshes, lakes, streams, and other wetlands. Occasionally they may be found feeding in pastures and fields. The White Ibis is also common along the entire Gulf coast and the Atlantic Coast to the Carolinas. After the breeding season, individuals may spread northward as far as the Great Lakes. It wasn't until recent years that the White Ibis was found to breed in Texas.

The White Ibis prefers to feed in freshwater marshes, shallow streams, lakes, and estuaries. They prefer salt marshes to fresh water. The favorite diet of the White Ibis consists of a whole variety of crustaceans including crabs, shrimp, and crayfish. A major part of their diet also includes fish, snakes, insects, and many small mollusks. As with most of the wading birds, they are opportunists and will take anything that is easily captured and swallowed.

The two-foot tall White Ibis is easily differentiated from the other white wading birds. The adult White Ibis has a red face. Its bill is long and curves downward in the typical ibis shape and is red with a black tip. Immature birds are dark above with a white belly. In flight, the White Ibis flies in typical 'V' formation or in a straight line. Because of the large number of birds in a flock, these formations may extend for over a mile. The tips of its white wings are black but the black area is not very extensive. Occasionally you will see a light-pink ibis that is probably a hybrid between the White Ibis and the pink Scarlet Ibis.

The White Ibis is extremely colonial and nests in dense colonies numbering into the thousands. Their nests are rather substantial and are found in shorter trees and shrubs. Material is added to the nest as the nesting season progresses. Nesting begins in March and extends into mid-spring. Two to three light blue-green eggs marked with various darker colors are incubated for three weeks. The young are fed regurgitated food and are able to leave the nest in about five weeks. The young will usually follow the main flocks as they go from one feeding area to another.

Although the population of White Ibis is not endangered, it is declining because of the loss of wetlands and areas for nesting.

White Ibis

ROSEATE SPOONBILL *Ajaia ajaja*

Probably no large wading bird causes such excitement as does the Roseate Spoonbill. From the beginner the first thing you hear is, "Look, a Flamingo!" However, flamingos are no longer common in the United States and even then were actually found only in Florida. Nevertheless, this bright pink bird is very striking. If the birds are close, the large spoon-shaped bill will give it away.

At just under three feet tall, the Roseate Spoonbill is easily identified. The adults are pink in color with a bright-orange tail and bright-pink accents on its upper wings and rump. The other common bird that may be confused with the Spoonbill is the Scarlet Ibis, although the Scarlet Ibis is a uniform pink over its entire body, including its legs. The neck and upper back of the Spoonbill are white. The Spoonbill's head is featherless except for on immature birds. Its most striking feature is the long flat bill that is spoon-shaped at the end—hence the name Spoonbill. Immature birds are predominately white, turning to the adult pink over two to three years.

These birds can commonly be seen wading in shallow water sweeping their spoon-shaped bill back and forth, feeding on aquatic organisms. They are most common in eastern Texas and along the Gulf coast. After breeding, the birds disperse all along the Gulf coast, even as far as Florida and up the Atlantic coastline. Breeding populations may be augmented by strays from the east and Mexico.

Nesting may begin as early as November in the southern part of the United States but not until April in the north. Usually three white eggs are laid in a very deep nest about twenty feet above the ground. Often the nests are in mixed colonies with egrets, herons, and ibis. The male usually brings the nesting material to the female who then builds the nest. The nest is probably the best built of the large wading birds. The eggs hatch in just over three weeks and the babies may take from five to six weeks to leave the nest. The young are fed regurgitated food from the parents and are able to move about the nest and tree in a few weeks.

Although the population has rebounded from the use of its feathers in hats and fans, there is still concern over these birds. The loss of habitat, especially in shallow waters, has shifted and even eliminated some populations. Draining of wetlands must be regulated and large expanses of wetlands must be preserved for these and many of the wetland species of the United States.

Roseate Spoonbill

BLACK- AND YELLOW-CROWNED NIGHT-HERON *Nycticorax nycticorax / Nyctanassa violacea*

These two herons are among the most interesting of the wading birds found in the southwest. As their name indicates, they feed extensively during the night, unlike the other herons and egrets. The Night-Herons have larger bills for their size and so are able to take advantage of larger prey.

Identifying these birds is relatively easy. They are both over two feet tall, rather chunky, and when seen during the day are usually roosting. The immature birds are brown with spots on their back and streaks on their front. It is difficult to distinguish the two types of young Night-Herons from each other, but the adult birds are easy. Both of the Night-Herons are gray overall. The Black-crowned Night-Heron has a black crown and a black back. The Yellow-crowned Night-Heron lacks the black back and has the yellow crown and a black chin that extends to the back of its head, producing the effect of a white patch behind its eye on the cheek.

The necks of the Night-Herons are not as long as other herons, possibly because their night-hunting habits make it less necessary to get as close to their prey. Both Night-Herons have plumes which arise from the head during breeding season. The legs of the adults are yellow or yellow-green except during breeding. Of the two, the Black-crowned Night-Heron is most likely to be seen. The Yellow-crowned Night-Heron is more secretive and not as abundant. Adult plum-age is not obtained in both species until the third year.

The Night-Herons feed on the same prey as the other herons but not necessarily the same species. Feeding at night, they are inclined to be more opportunistic, taking just about anything living including small mammals, birds, and a whole host of amphibians. The main diet, of course, is fish and aquatic invertebrates.

The Black-crowned Night-Heron can be found throughout the southwest in the correct habitat, whereas the Yellow-crowned Night-Heron is found in east Texas and the Gulf coast. Both are more abundant when breeding birds from the north arrive. Their preferred habitat is shrubby wooded shorelines where they can creep and feed along near the water's edge. If they feed during the day, they will wade in shallow water especially near mangroves.

Their eggs are a light blue-green and are laid in a loose platform of sticks and twigs. Their nests are more securely hidden than those of the other herons. The eggs hatch after about three weeks and the adults feed the young partially digested to small undigested food. Feeding occurs at dawn, dusk, and throughout the night.

These birds are quite striking and you can see them readily if you look in trees, mangroves, and shrubs in wet areas. In populated areas, they may forage during the day along with other herons.

Top: Yellow-crowned Night-Heron
Bottom: Black-crowned Night-heron

MALLARD *Anas platyrhynchos*

Normally considered a duck of the north, the Mallard is found throughout the southwest, especially during the winter months as northern migrating birds invade the area. Although not generally considered a breeding bird in the southwest, the Mallard does breed occasionally in some parts of California, Arizona, and Texas. Wild Mallards can be found in the southwest at all times of the year. The greatest influx of birds comes after the waters of the north have frozen solid in November and December.

Most Mallards return north just as the ice leaves the lakes and streams to lay eggs and produce a single brood of ducklings. Each year the number of Mallards spending the winter in the southwest varies. Influencing the numbers is the spring hatch, hunting pressure along the migration route, and the severity of the winter, both timing and temperature.

Identifying the Mallard is relatively easy. The male is also called a "Green Head" because his head is entirely green. Its bill is yellow or greenish-yellow and the green is bordered by a band of white. It is the only duck with these characteristics. If the head of the Mallard were not striking enough, the male has a bright-mahogany breast with gray feathers on its sides. Its tail is black-and-white with a few curled feathers on the top. Its back is light-brown. The female is not as colorful, being predominately a mottled brown with an orange-yellow bill with some black on it. Both sexes have orange feet and a bright-blue speculum that is bordered on the top and bottom with a white stripe. This bright-blue area is most evident in flight with a little showing as they sit or swim.

Along the gulf coat of Texas, the Mottled Duck, although rare, may be confused with the female Mallard. The main distinguishing feature of the Mottled Duck is the yellow bill which has no other markings.

The Mallard is a dabbling duck; it does the bulk of its feeding on the surface of the water. The Mallard feeds with its head underwater, sifting the bottom for vegetation, small invertebrates and crustaceans. In deeper water, it will "tip up" until the entire front of its body is underwater. In agricultural lands it has adapted well to grains of all types.

During the winter months the female picks her mate and returns to the area in which she was reared, taking him with her.

Mallard
Top: Female Bottom: Male

BLUE-WINGED TEAL *Anas discors*

One of the smallest ducks to visit the southwest is the Blue-winged Teal. The Blue-winged Teal also spends from late August to the following May in Florida. However, most birds arrive in early fall and leave by late March of the following year. This little duck can be found throughout the southwest where there is water. The only place this bird is extremely rare is in the deserts of Arizona and similar habitats.

Besides its small size, the Blue-winged Teal is quite easy to identify. The male has a gray head, black forehead, and prominent white moon-shaped crescent in front of the eye which follows the front of the head from the top to bottom. The forehead is a darker gray. The body of both the male and female is brown with specks of black. Both have a bright-green speculum with sky-blue wing patches from the speculum to the forewing, which are noticeable in flight. The male Blue-winged Teal has a black rear with a prominent white spot on its lower body in front of the black area.

Nesting is erratic in the southwest. The female builds a nest in grass in order to hide it. The nest is constructed not far from water with whatever plant materials are available, usually grasses, sedges and cattails. After a clutch of about twelve to fifteen cream-colored eggs is laid, down from the hen is added to the nest. Incubation lasts just short of four weeks.

About a day after the ducklings dry, the hen will lead them to water where food and protection is more readily available. The ducklings remain with the hen until they begin to fly and may even migrate with the hen in family groups. The male abandons the female after the eggs begin to hatch and goes through a molt whereupon it resembles the immature and female birds until well into the fall.

One of the dabbling ducks, the Blue-winged Teal feeds in shallow water, preferring freshwater. The Blue-winged Teal feeds on aquatic vegetation from the surface and the soft bottom mud, rarely diving below the water with its entire body. Most of its food consists of seeds and small aquatic plants, but the Blue-winged Teal will also take small aquatic insects, crustaceans, and snails. Agricultural and natural seeds are also an important part of the diet of this small duck. After the harvest season, you may see numerous birds landing in fields to glean spilled corn, oats, rice, or any grain.

Blue-winged Teal
Top: Male Bottom: Female

GADWALL *Anas strepera*

From a distance, the Gadwall is a plain-looking duck. The female Gadwell, like the female Mallard, is a mixture of browns and grays. The male is a soft-gray overall with a fawn head and a striking black rump. The male's black bill is noticeable against the fawn head. In flight, the Gadwall has white wing patches (speculum) on the trailing edge of its wings which are normally hidden when not in flight. It is almost easier to identify this bird because of its lack of bright colors, especially when combined with its dark rump. In both sexes the feet are yellow. At about twenty inches long, the Gadwall is smaller than the Mallard.

The Gadwall is a dabbling duck, tipping up to feed in shallow water. The Gadwall feeds mainly on aquatic plants but will not pass up insects and small crustaceans. During the migratory season the Gadwall will also eat seeds and grains. The Gadwall winters in the southwest and breeds in the prairie states up into Canada. It can be found in lakes, ponds, marshes, and less commonly on the Gulf and its estuaries. Most often it is associated with other dabblers such as the Mallard, Shoveler, Black Duck, and Teal.

In the breeding areas, it prefers to place its nest in dense vegetation near water. The hen builds the nests and incubates the eggs alone. About a dozen white eggs are laid over a two week period late in the spring or early summer. The Gadwall's nest can be a dump nest for ducks which have yet to build a nest but which are already laying eggs. Incubation takes about four weeks. The young can fly in about eight weeks and will stay together with the hen as family unit into the migratory season. The Gadwall breeds in parts of New Mexico and California.

Gadwall
Top: Female Bottom: Male

NORTHERN PINTAIL *Anas acuta*

The Northern Pintail is one of the most popular ducks for woodcarvers and painters because of its elegant look and, of course, its "pen" or "pin" tail. As in most ducks, the hen Pintail is a nondescript mottled brown overall, similar to the female Mallard. At just over two feet in length, the Northern Pintail is not quite as large as a Mallard but it may appear larger because it is so slender and sleek- looking. The drake Pintail has a striking white breast that extends in a slender line or point into the dark head. Its body is a delicately-penciled gray with a white patch on the side of its rump culminating in the long pin-shaped tail. In flight, its wings show a brown speculum trailing to a soft white edge.

In the southwest, the Pintail is a winter resident, spending the season in shallow ponds, backwaters, flooded farm fields, estuaries, and lakes. Being a dabbler, it is not very common on the Gulf or the ocean. It can be quite abundant during the winter season, feeding on harvested rice and corn fields. During the winter, its food is almost entirely seeds and grains.

In the Texas Panhandle and Colorado, the Pintail can be a breeding species. As in the Mallards, pairing occurs during the winter although some pairing can continue during migration and even in the nesting territories. Nesting begins in early spring with the hen building the nest and laying from six to twelve pale-olive eggs. The nest is usually built on dry land near water but, as with Mallards and many other ducks, they may place their nest as far as a half mile away from water. The male doesn't help with any of the rearing after incubation begins. The nest is constructed of grasses and other plant material and lined with down from the hen's breast. At hatching, the ducklings quickly dry off and a few hours later they are able to follow mom to the relative safety of water.

This journey can be one of the most hazardous for the ducklings as they can only protect themselves by hiding, sometimes so well that even mom isn't able to round them up to continue their journey. Once on the water, the young are able to feed themselves and can dive to hide. The hen keeps them together and watches for danger. On the water, two of the most successful predators are the snapping turtle and large fish like the northern pike and largemouth bass. The young are able to fly at about seven weeks in the southwest but in the north it takes a bit longer.

Ice is usually the determining factor in the departure of the last birds. Spring migration occurs as soon as northern waters become free of ice. The Pintail population is affected by hunting but more importantly by the weather conditions during the nesting season. Drought can severely affect fall populations. Populations have also declined from the 1950s due to habitat loss in the nesting areas.

Northern Pintail
Top: Female Bottom: Male

BLACK-BELLIED WHISTLING-DUCK

Dendrocygna autumnalis

Common only on the coast of Texas and in parts of Arizona, the Black-bellied Whistling-Duck can however be found in pockets in every southwestern state. Except for in Texas, this bird usually leaves the southwest for the winter, but may remain if conditions are favorable.

The Black-bellied Whistling-Duck is striking at nearly two feet tall and standing erect like a goose. Because it nests in trees, it is called a tree duck. Its legs are long and are bright pink. Its bill is a bright lipstick-red. Its head has gray patches on the side with a burnt-orange or rust color down its breast and back. Its wings are white and its belly is black. In flight, the bright-white forewings and black belly are quite prominent.

The Black-bellied Whistling-Duck prefers wooded wetlands and ponds surrounded by trees. They have adapted well to city parks where trees and ponds are available. These ducks are gregarious and may be found in large groups scrounging food from people along ponds and walkways in the parks.

Similar to Canada Geese, the Black-bellied Whistling-Duck appears to mate for life. Occasionally these birds will nest in loose groups or colonies, but the normal place for nest building is in a tree cavity or hollow. They have adapted well to nest boxes with a layer of wood chips in the bottom. The adults line the chips with down. It also nests on the ground

if necessary. Their nests are usually dry, close to water, and well-hidden in shrubs or tall vegetation. Its nest is lined with soft grasses and other plant material. A nest on the ground may become a "dump" nest and accumulate as many as four or five dozen eggs. Nests with this many eggs are usually not very successful.

Both parents share in the incubation which lasts about four weeks. As in the Wood Ducks, the young have sharp toenails which enable them to climb out of the deep nest cavity. When building a nest box make sure that the front of the inside of the box is rough or has hardware cloth attached to give the ducklings a toehold. The young are able to follow both adults after a few days and are tended by both parents. The young are able to take care of themselves after a couple of months.

These ducks are gregarious and feed in loose flocks in fields and on farmlands as well as in shallow aquatic areas. Their main diet is seeds and vegetation but they won't pass up any invertebrate although they rarely eat fish. During the fall, large groups of these birds may forage in farm fields for grain and actually look like flocks of small geese from a distance.

The Black-bellied Whistling-Duck has increased in population over the last forty or fifty years and has increased its range northward and westward. The greatest growth appears to be in Arizona.

Black-bellied Whistling-Duck

BLACK AND TURKEY VULTURE

Coragyps atratus / Cathartes aura

These two vultures are the most common vultures in North America. The Black Vulture and Turkey Vulture are both large and black, with the Black Vulture being the smaller of the two. With their wingspan of five or six feet, these birds are often mistaken for eagles. Vultures have small heads which are devoid of feathers—which most likely helps keep their head clean when they feed on rotting carcasses. The material from the carcasses dries up and falls off the bare skin of the head and upper neck.

The Vulture's bill is sharply hooked (as in many raptors) but instead of using its bill to capture prey it uses it to tear apart the decaying bodies of its prey. Vultures have a good sense of smell, unusual for many birds, which helps them locate carrion from great distances. The Black Vulture has a less sensitive sense of smell than the Turkey Vulture. Road kills have become a significant part of these two vultures' diet.

These two vultures are relatively easy to tell apart. The head of the adult Turkey Vulture is red in color, whereas the Black Vulture's is a dark-gray. The miniature Turkey Vulture is also gray. In soaring flight, the Turkey Vulture keeps its wings at an angle to its body making it appear like the letter 'V' from the ground. The Turkey Vulture also tips from side to side in flight so the 'V' is quite evident. The Black Vulture keeps its wings parallel to the ground, presenting a straight line from wing tip to wing tip. Since both Vultures have small heads, the flight silhouette appears almost headless. In flight, the tail of the Black Vulture is very short and squared off at the end. Its legs stretch back to the end of its tail and, in some cases, may extend beyond its tail. This characteristic is never true in the case of the Turkey Vulture.

The wing patterns are also used to differentiate these two birds. The Black Vulture's shorter wings have white patches at the ends, whereas the Turkey Vulture has light patterns on the entire trailing edge of the wings from primaries to the body. Both species are more prevalent during the winter with the influx of individuals from the north.

Both vultures are communal in their roosting habits and you may find whole trees full of these birds in the early morning before the warm air thermals take them away to feed. The Turkey Vulture is common over the entire southwest but the Black Vulture is only sporadically found. The Black Vulture is most common in east Texas but is increasing in numbers as far west as Arizona.

Turkey Vulture (second from top in flight and full picture)
Black Vulture (top in flight) and Head (left center)

SWAINSON'S HAWK *Buteo swainsoni*

Swainson's Hawk is probably one of the most common hawks found in the southwest. The only place it isn't common is in southern California and the extreme northeastern part of Texas. During the winter, the southwest is almost devoid of these birds as they migrate southward as far as Argentina. It nests northward as far as southern Canada.

Swainson's Hawk spends much of its time over open grasslands and scrub lands where it feeds on lizards, small mammals, small birds, and insects. If you see a large concentration of hawks in the evening, you may wish to watch until dusk to see if a bat cave is nearby. Some caves contain millions of bats which leave at dusk in huge numbers making them easy prey for a short time. During late summer, Swainson's Hawk enjoys a diet of insects.

At about twenty inches tall and with a wingspan of about four feet, Swainson's Hawk is not extremely large. This buteo has broad wings that are a bit more pointed than others of its kind. The identifying characteristic to look for is the dark-brown breast band from its neck downward. Its primary and flight feathers contrast with its light-buff wing linings. In its dark phase, the opposite is true: its flight feathers, although still dark, are lighter than the wing linings. Similar to the Zone-tailed Hawk and vultures, its wings are often held above the horizontal while soaring, giving it a slight 'V' shape. Its light-gray tail is banded with a heavier band near the outer edge.

Nesting occurs in the early spring in open groves of trees. A large tree is selected and the nest is usually built about ten to thirty feet above the ground. The nest is constructed of twigs and grasses. Swainson's Hawk will often use its own old nests or those of owls or magpies. Normally the three or four bluish-white eggs are incubated solely by the female, who is fed by the male during that time. Incubation takes about five weeks during which both parents will feed the young. The female will remain with the young as long as they need protection, but as they get older she will venture from the nest to forage and bring food. In six or seven weeks the young will leave the nest but remain as a family group until migration.

Populations have declined, especially in California, probably due to pesticides or habitat loss. Spring migration can be quite spectacular when large "kettles" of these hawks, mixed with others, circle overhead riding the thermal winds upwards until they are invisible. They then set their wings and glide downward to the north only to catch yet another thermal and rise again. Kettles of several thousand hawks can occasionally be seen.

Swainson's Hawk

FERRUGINOUS HAWK *Buteo regalis*

Another common southwestern buteo is the Ferruginous Hawk. This buteo nests in the western United States north into Canada and south into the southwest. Many continue south into Mexico. In the winter months, the Ferruginous Hawk can be found in open areas of desert, scrub, and prairies except in east Texas. It has also adapted well to the presence of man, frequenting pasture land as well as cultivated and fallow fields.

The Ferruginous Hawk stands about two feet tall and has a wingspan of nearly four-and-a-half feet, making it slightly larger than the Red-shouldered Hawk. Its back and upper wings are a rusty-red, similar to the Red- shouldered Hawk, except the red is more extensive. Its head is fairly light and its underside is whitish with a dark crescent shape prominent at the "wrists." Its tail is a very pale-rust to almost white, the rust being more noticeable. From above, the base of the primary feathers are white creating a window past the "knuckles." The feathers on its legs are rust-colored and are quite prominent in flight.

Like the Rough-legged Hawk, the Ferruginous Hawk hovers when hunting. It also sits on the ground waiting for a rodent to leave its burrow. The main diet of the Ferruginous Hawk is rabbits, mice, and shrews but it will also take birds, lizards, snakes, and large insects.

Nesting occurs in the tops of fairly large trees, normally fifteen to fifty feet above the ground except in areas where tall trees are at a premium. Its nest is composed of sticks and twigs and lined with finer materials. It has been reported that when the buffalo were abundant their bones and dung were primarily used for nesting materials. Nests are reused and old owl and crow nests may be refurbished.

Four to six pale-blue eggs are laid and the female does most of the incubation. The male tends to her food needs during the four-and-a-half weeks it takes the eggs to hatch. As the young get older, the female will leave them to forage and the young take their maiden flight in about seven weeks. Family groups may stay in the same area over the winter.

This hawk is declining over most of its range largely due to past hunting pressure and habitat loss. The southwest is one of the most reliable places to see this hawk, especially during the winter.

Ferruginous Hawk

HARRIS' HAWK *Parabuteo unicinctus*

Harris' Hawk is probably one of the most striking and colorful hawks the United States has to offer outside the American Kestrel. Found only in the southwest, it is a treat to see and is sought out by many birders. Harris' Hawk is found only in southern Texas, southeast New Mexico, and southern Arizona. Previously nesting only in extreme southern California, reintroduction is being attempted with some success.

Harris' Hawk is a rich dark-brown (almost black) all over with mahogany shoulder patches and legs. Its wing linings to the "knuckle" are mahogany. In flight, its tail has a wide black band near the end and a white narrow tip. Its upper and lower rump are white, making for a spectacular contrast. This hawk is not large at only twenty-one inches long and with a wingspan of just under four feet.

Harris' Hawk can be found in semi-arid lands of the southwest. A very social bird, you may find one or more hunting together in scattered scrub lands. Where perching places are at a premium, they have been known to sit one atop the other, sometimes several on one cactus or tree stub. It's quite a sight to see; something like a cheerleading pyramid.

In the desert scrub and open scrub lands, Harris' Hawk feeds upon small mammals, birds, lizards, snakes, and large insects. It will also take larger mammals up to the size of a rabbit. It is a extremely powerful flyer and similar to the Cooper's and Sharp-shinned Hawk, it will often pursue its prey into dense mesquite and cactus, sometimes running across the ground. Harris' Hawk has adapted well to feeding in suburbia where there is mature vegetation.

This hawk nests in smaller trees, larger shrubs, and in the crotches of the saguaro cactus at about twelve to twenty feet above the ground. Its nest is made of sticks and is fairly bulky. It is lined with finer material and new-leaved twigs are added during the nesting cycle. Both the male and female take care of the nest and occasionally an additional male may accompany the group. The trio seems to work out well. Two or three broods are produced each year and the young of a previous batch may attend a subsequent brood. Families may stay together during non-nesting seasons. Usually four pale-blue to white eggs are laid and incubated primarily by the female with the male feeding her during that time. Incubation takes a little over four to five weeks. In another six weeks the young are able to leave the nest.

Populations have recently stabilized although they are more abundant further north in the Colorado River Valley and into California. Earlier hunting pressure may be one reason for the lack of birds and more recently the use of this extremely attractive bird for falconry may be a cause of concern.

Harris' Hawk

RED-SHOULDERED HAWK   *Buteo lineatus*

The Red-shouldered Hawk is a common breeding hawk throughout central and eastern Texas as well as parts of southern California in the correct habitat. This hawk is smaller than the Red-tailed Hawk. The Red-shouldered Hawk stands about eighteen to twenty inches tall and is not as robust in stature as the Red-tailed Hawk. The breast of the Red-shouldered Hawk is rusty-red. Its shoulder has a dark-red patch which is not always easy to distinguish. However, its red shoulders are quite evident when seen from above or when the bird is twisting and turning in flight. Its tail is black with narrow white bands which appear as alternate bands of narrow white and broad black. The head is dark and the legs are yellow. A variety of Red-shouldered Hawk that is smaller and lighter in color appears in southern Florida.

Wet forests and flood plain forests with mature canopies near wetlands are the preferred habitat for this hawk. The diet of the Red-shouldered Hawk is reptiles and amphibians. The Red-shouldered Hawk is one of the best snake-capturing hawks in the southwest. Sometimes it will bring more than a half dozen snakes to the nest each day. In the southwest, lizards make up a good portion of its diet but are less important further north. The Red-shouldered Hawk is also very proficient at capturing frogs, insects, and crayfish. At certain times of the year rodents are a good portion of its diet.

Nests are usually built in the heavy crotch of tall trees. They are substantial and are built from sticks, twigs, and other plant materials. The nest is lined with finer material such as grasses, Spanish moss, and green vegetation. The nest is added to as incubation progresses. Nests are often used over and over again, or at least every couple of years if successful nesting has occurred.

Three and sometimes four eggs are laid in the nest in January and incubated for four weeks. The eggs are off-white with brown markings. The young are attended by both parents. The young are fed bits of prey at first but as they become older they are brought whole frogs and snakes to tear apart and devour. At certain times of the day an adult bird may shelter the young from the hot sun if the nest is open from above. The young are able to leave the nest in about six weeks. Nesting has become a prime consideration for these birds and they have become somewhat adapted to man if the proper nesting trees are available.

Red-shouldered Hawk

OSPREY *Pandion haliaetus*

Recovering from low populations in the middle of this century, the Osprey has become quite abundant during the winter in Texas where open water is prevalent. The Osprey can also be found in California and breeds locally in Arizona, California, New Mexico, Colorado, and Utah. The "Fish Hawk," as it is many times called, is the most proficient of the fish-capturing birds of prey. It can be seen hovering above a body of water. The Osprey dives feet first into the water and usually comes up with a fairly large fish.

The talons of this bird of prey are highly maneuverable and when it transports a large fish, the Osprey carries it parallel to its body so the length of the fish is in line with its body with the head usually pointing forward. This characteristic helps distinguish the Osprey from the Bald Eagle. The undersides of the Osprey differ from the Bald Eagle as well. The Osprey has a white front except for its tail. The Bald Eagle is dark on the front and its tail is white. The head of the Osprey is white except for a wide dark-brown eye-stripe, which also helps separate it from the Bald Eagle. The upper part of the body, wings, and tail are dark-brown overall and its tail has faint bands running across it. A band of brown specks runs across the bottom of its neck. One of the most noticeable features of the Osprey in flight are the black "knuckles"—dark patches at the bend in the

wing which makes the bend appear extremely pronounced.

The Osprey has taken readily to manmade towers and nest platforms, especially those placed directly in the water. Nests that the birds build for themselves may be on telephone or utility poles, dead trees, or other high areas. The nests are made of assorted materials. Since these nests are used for years they may become quite large, similar to the Bald Eagle's nests. These birds are not terribly territorial and the large nests may be quite close to each other.

Nesting occurs during late spring and often the same successful site will be used again and again. Usually three eggs are placed in the nest and incubation begins immediately, thereby causing the chicks to hatch a few days apart. Incubation lasts about five weeks. The young are fed regurgitated food from the male for the first week or so, then the female will tear apart fish for the chicks. The Osprey chicks will remain in the nest for about seven weeks before leaving to feed with the parents.

In the southwest, the Osprey has become a bird of special concern and the number of nest platforms placed out on lakes and marshes has been increased. Wetland preservation is probably the most prudent way to ensure the survival of this fish-eating raptor.

Osprey

NORTHERN BOBWHITE *Colinus virginianus*

Commonly called the "Quail" or "Bobwhite Quail," this bird gets its name from its loud call of *bob bob white*! About nine inches tall, the Bobwhite is a reddish-brown ground-feeding bird. Its body is heavily mottled with crescents on each feather. Its head has a white eye-stripe with a white throat in the male and a buff-colored throat in the female. Both sexes may exhibit a crown when excited but the male's crest is more pronounced and darker than the female's. Preferring to run instead of fly, the Bobwhite can be seen scurrying about brushy areas. When surprised the Bobwhite will explode in a unnerving bombshell of rapid wing beats.

The Northern Bobwhite is found throughout Texas, eastern New Mexico, and northward in open forests, brushy areas, fields, and marginal agricultural areas, primarily cattle pastures. Except during breeding, the Northern Bobwhites will stay together in a group called a "covey." Most coveys are family groupings until fall when some will combine to make larger coveys.

In the southwest, as in much of the south, the Bobwhite Quail is a game bird and is hunted extensively, usually with English Pointers. In restaurants, the Quail offered on the menus have been farm-raised as most states do not allow game to be sold.

The female builds a nest with a hood over it and a side entrance. The nest is made from grasses and fine vegetation. Nesting begins in February with fourteen to fifteen eggs being laid. Incubation takes about three-and-a-half weeks with the chicks able to follow the female after drying out. The chicks are attended by both parents and are about the size of large bumblebees. Young quail chicks are very vulnerable and are brooded by the female frequently during the cooler parts of the day.

Young quail will go through a series of molts before taking on the adult plumage. The young will be capable of short quick flights in about four weeks. It is at this time that some merging of larger coveys occurs. When at rest, especially at night, the members of the covey sleep with their heads pointing outward, probably for protection. If startled they will literally explode in all directions of the circle. A telltale sign of roosting coveys is an extensive group of black-and-white droppings.

The adult and young birds eat a variety of different types of food. Young insects are a major part of the diet but seeds, berries, and other invertebrates are all eaten extensively.

Northern Bobwhite

WILD TURKEY *Meleagris gallopavo*

The Wild Turkey is the largest game bird in the southwest as well as the rest of the United States. The Wild Turkey is smaller than the domestic turkey. It resembles the domestic Bronze Turkey because of the bronze-colored iridescent sheen of its dark feathers which makes this bird extremely beautiful when viewed up close. Standing almost four feet tall, the male is larger than the female and sports a red-and-blue featherless head which becomes brightly colored when in courtship display. The beak sports a knob of flesh called a "snerd" which becomes long and flashy during courtship antics. The size of the "snerd" can become ten times longer than when in a non-excited stage. The male also has a tuft of feathers which is called a "beard." This tuft of feathers is more like a small horsetail hanging down from the center of the breast. Occasionally the female may have a beard. Females are about a foot shorter and do not have the brightly-colored head.

The Wild Turkey can be found in forested wild areas. Its population is increasing in the correct habitat. In the forest it forages on seeds, nuts, and insects. In some areas it has adapted well to agricultural fields that are adjacent to wild forested areas. In the northern part of the United States, as well as the southwest, the agricultural areas are becoming a more important part of the Wild Turkey's habitat.

During the early spring the male turkeys strut about with their tails spread out like the proverbial Thanksgiving turkey and gobble to attract or locate females. This gobbling normally occurs during the early dawn hours. During March the female scrapes out a hidden nest and lines it sparsely with some leaves and vegetation. She will normally lay less than a dozen eggs but some northern broods may be one or two larger.

Incubation of the buff-colored eggs which are marked with light brown lasts about four weeks. The young are precocial and after drying for about a day they are able to leave the nest with the female. For the first part of the immature birds' life they forage in grassy fields for insects. Females with broods of different ages may form loose groups which can be quite impressive. To see a group of three or four hens with chicks of four different ages is quite a sight. Just seeing forty birds together is in itself remarkable.

The Wild Turkey can be seen in oak wood lots, pine forests, and state game areas and parks. In the early dawn hours they can be found roosting in trees. Care should be taken not to confuse them with vultures. During the day, the Wild Turkey feeds in the forests or edges of fields.

Wild Turkey

GAMBEL'S QUAIL AND SCALED QUAIL
Callipepla gambelii / Callipepla squamata

In the desert scrub lands of the south west and at the edge of suburbia, the call of the Gambel's Quail is a part of the evening and morning sounds. The most striking part of this foot high bird is the "top knot" on its head that ends in a tear shape. It has a black face bordered in white and the crown is a rich mahogany. Its overall body is a grayish-green with mahogany sides. Its unmarked belly and lower breast are buff with a black spot on the lower belly. In California this bird is replaced by the California Quail.

The Scaled Quail is smaller than Gambel's Quail by a couple inches and is not as brightly marked. The Scaled Quail can be found over most of New Mexico, parts of Arizona, western Texas, and parts of Colorado. The habitat preferred by the Scaled Quail is shrubby open country. The Scaled Quail is just as its name suggests, marked with scales over its buff brown body. It does sport a top knot but it is just a short tuft reminiscent of a Cardinal's. Its scaled underside is much more buff-colored than its back.

In the correct habitats they can be attracted to feeders. Both quail feed mainly on seeds and berries but will take insects when available. Insects become a greater part of their diet when they are rearing young, probably for the increased protein. Of the two, the Scaled Quail eats more insects than Gambel's Quail, possibly because of their greater availability in the grassy areas as opposed to a more arid habitat.

Breeding and nesting are similar with the male calling to attract a female. Usually a dozen or more eggs are laid in a depression lined with grasses and other soft vegetation. In both cases the female attends to incubation which takes about three weeks. When the young are dry they are able to follow the parents who teach them to feed and watch for predators. After a couple of weeks the young grow some primary flight feathers and are able to fly short distances to escape predators.The family will stay together in a covey, and some family groups may combine for the winter.

As spring arrives the coveys break up into breeding pairs and territories. Populations of these birds seem to be stable overall but fluctuate with the success of breeding in dry or wet years. The Scaled Quail seems to have adapted to some agricultural areas.

Top: Gambel's Quail
Bottom: Scaled Quail

WHOOPING CRANE AND SANDHILL CRANE

Grus americana / Grus canadensis

The Whooping Crane is probably one of the most sought after birds in the southwest. Both the Sandhill Crane and Whooping Crane are found in the southwest only during the winter. The Whooping Crane is normally only found in Aransas National Wildlife Refuge in Texas and Bosque del Apache Refuge in New Mexico. The Whooping Crane is a success story, having been brought back from near extinction to well over two hundred birds today, both free and captive.

The Whooping Crane stands about four-and-half-feet tall and has a wingspan of just under eight feet. It is white overall with black primary feathers visible while in flight. When standing or walking its primaries are hidden. Its face is red with a red crown. Young birds are a buff color until mature plumage is obtained. The Whooping Crane gets its name from the whooping call it makes during the mating dance when it throws grasses and twigs into the air and bows and parades around. Most of the crane species have involved mating rituals.

The Whooping Crane nests in Canada at Wood Buffalo National Park and that population winters in Texas. Because of hunting, the Whooping Crane population dropped to fifteen. Even today the long migration from northern Canada to Texas is fraught with hazards ranging from ignorant hunters to weather and power lines. Today the wintering flock of free birds migrating to Texas is approaching two hundred. An attempt to establish a breeding area in the United States seems to have met with little success. Whooping Crane eggs were put under Sandhill Cranes and although they were successful in rearing the chicks and getting them to migrate to New Mexico, a problem arose because the chicks became so imprinted on the Sandhill Crane they wouldn't mate later with other Whooping Crane chicks.

Sandhill Cranes are gray overall, lighter on their neck with a red crown and forehead. As in the Whooping Crane their primaries are a bit darker but do not show the black contrast of the Whooping Crane. Probably the most identifying characteristic of the Sandhill Crane is its call, a rattling *karroo karroo karroo* which can be heard from a long distance. Once learned this call will not be forgotten.

The Sandhill is quite abundant although hunting and habitat destruction have caused some populations to decrease. Fall and spring migrations are very impressive when literally thousands migrate together. In the southwest they frequent marshes and open fields. They forage over grain fields and are opportunistic in their eating habits, eating primarily grains and insects but not passing up a frog, tadpole, or fish when available.

Most populations winter in Texas and New Mexico although a small population winters in southern California.

Left: Whooping Crane
Right: Sandhill Crane

AMERICAN COOT *Fulica americana*

Most abundant during the winter, the American Coot nests in the southwest, primarily in the interior on freshwater marshes, lakes, ponds, and backwaters of rivers. The "Mud Hen," as it is sometimes called, is common in the southwest. The population is heavily augmented during the winter from northern populations, making this bird one of the most abundant in open water areas. The American Coot is similar in shape to that of the Purple and Common Gallinules, except that it is more duck-shaped and tends to frequent open water.

The American Coot is a dark-gray overall with an almost black head. The American Coot has a white bill and white rump patch that appears on each side of its rump.The upper part of its bill or shield is a deep-red or orange, almost appearing as a knob. Occasionally an American Coot may exhibit a whitish shield, which may indicate that it is a Caribbean Coot or hybrid. However, further studies have shown that many Coots exhibit the white shield. In flight, the American Coot exhibits narrow white trailing edges on its wings. The toes of the American Coot are lobed, almost appearing webbed, but they are still divided like the foot of the chicken. Perhaps this is one reason it is called "mud hen." The legs in the adults are yellow-green and those of the immature birds are dark.

Usually feeding in groups, the American Coot's diet is heavily con-centrated on aquatic vegetation and it is therefore usually found in shallow water. Although it feeds primarily on plants, the Coot will also eat aquatic insects, crustaceans, and snails. The American Coot is a good swimmer and can also catch fish, tadpoles, and other fast swimmers. The American Coot is not above stealing food from other water birds. In the north, some Coots will stay as long as the water remains unfrozen, but the bulk of them migrate to the south and southwest where they can reach huge populations, even becoming a problem by leaving huge amounts of tell-tale signs along banks of park and golf course lakes.

Nests are placed in areas of emerging vegetation and a floating platform of vegetation is anchored around the nest. Dummy nests may be made, with only one used for egg-laying. The others may be used for courting or resting with newly-hatched young. About ten buff-colored eggs marked with brown are laid and incubation takes three-and-a-half weeks. Nesting may begin in March and those nests that are successful may allow a second brood. Research indicates that the American Coot can recognize its eggs from those of a duck that wishes to parasitize the nest with its own eggs.

American Coot

COMMON MOORHEN   *Gallinula chloropus*

The Common Moorhen, or Common Gallinule as it was previously called, is quite abundant in the wetlands throughout east Texas, southern New Mexico, Arizona, and California, especially the interior. It can be found in freshwater marshes, ponds, lake edges, and less commonly, in brackish and saltwater areas. It prefers the edges of the water where it can make use of vegetation in which to hide and feed. Occasionally, the Common Moorhen can be found swimming in the open water.

The Common Moorhen is relatively large at just over a foot tall and is not terribly afraid of humans. This chicken-like bird can easily be seen in most natural areas and can be studied if it is not approached too closely. Although not as brightly-colored as the Purple Gallinule, the Common Moorhen is quite a handsome bird. About fourteen inches tall, the Common Moorhen stands erect like the barnyard chicken and has large feet, similar to the chicken. Actually, the toes of the Common Moorhen are quite a bit longer which aids it in walking over the marsh vegetation where it feeds.

The bird is slate-black over its front with a darker head and neck. Its back is olive-brown. The most striking and easily identified characteristic is the red facial shield that runs from its bill to its forehead. Its bill is red with a yellow tip. Its flanks have a white stripe and its under-tail feathers are white. It flicks its tail around as it walks about searching for food. Its legs and toes are yellow with a reddish band on its legs above the uppermost joint. The rare Purple Gallinule is similar, except quite purple in color and its forehead shield is blue above the red bill.

While swimming, the Common Gallinule pushes its head forward as if pumping its body along with the head push. The Common Moorhen eats a variety of marsh plants as well as seeds, insects, crustaceans, and small mollusks. During the season, berries can be a substantial part of the Common Moorhen's diet. Nests are usually constructed in the water on a mound or a floating mat and are constructed of marsh vegetation, usually cattails and reeds. Occasionally the nest will be constructed in shrubs or on land, but this allows more predation of the nest to occur.

The buff-colored eggs are marked with brown and are laid during late winter to early spring. Eight to twelve eggs are laid in the nest and incubation lasts about three weeks. In Florida and parts of the south, two broods are not uncommon with the juveniles from the first brood assisting with the second brood. The chicks are all black and able to leave the nest when dried.

Common Moorhen

CLAPPER RAIL *Rallus longirostris*

Rails are short stocky marsh birds that wade about in the reeds, cattails, and grasses seeking insects and seclusion. Because of their habits they are quite secretive and most people only know them by their voices. The Clapper Rail is one of the largest, standing at sixteen inches high. The Clapper Rail has gray legs and a tan and gray body. Its breast is rust-tan with barring along its flanks. Its bill is long and slightly decurved with a relatively heavy base. Its body is compressed laterally allowing it to slide through the reeds and cattails of the marshes it frequents. When feeding or moving about it does so in jerky movements while twitching its tail back and forth, a characteristic of many rails. Often it is overlooked because it blends in so well with the vegetation.

The Clapper Rail's call, *cac cac cac cac cac*, is a cackle of notes that increase in frequency and then slow down. It often continues ten to fourteen times in a row. The calls, which are the best way to locate this bird, are more likely to be heard in the evening and morning hours.

In the southwest, the Clapper Rail is found in the salt marshes of Texas and California. In some local situations it can be found in brackish water as well in some very local freshwater areas of the Colorado River basin and the Salton Sea.

The diet of the Clapper Rail is predominately insects and crustaceans. It will also eat small fish, frogs, tadpoles, and mollusks. Although mainly carnivorous upon occasion it eats seeds and aquatic vegetation.

Both sexes build a nest of aquatic grasses and sedges above the high tide line. Often the nest has a "roof" built over it of vegetation woven through standing plants. Up to twelve eggs are commonly laid in the nest ranging in color from pale-cream to light-olive and marked with blotches of brown or gray. Incubation takes three weeks and is shared by both parents. After drying, the downy black chicks follow the parents and learn to feed. They are quite adept at hiding and diving if threatened. Young birds are able to fly at ten weeks.

Although the eastern population seems to be stable, the Clapper Rails of the southwest are in serious danger. Most likely the decline has been due to loss of habitat.

Clapper Rail

AMERICAN OYSTERCATCHER
Haematopus palliatus

Entirely a bird of the coasts, the American Oystercatcher is more abundant on the Gulf coast than the Pacific coast. Although its populations have decreased greatly since the turn of the century, the American Oystercatcher seems to be holding its own, especially on the Gulf coast. It breeds northward almost to Cape Cod. The population along the Gulf coast is spotty with most breeding populations located in Texas.

This rather large-bodied shorebird is about a foot-and-a-half tall and is quite striking if you see it feeding along the coasts of Texas and California. The most noticeable feature of this noisy shorebird is its large red-orange bill which is flattened to allow it to pry apart the shells of mollusks. The Oystercatcher has a black head with yellow eyes surrounded by a red eye-ring. The back of the Oystercatcher is dark-brown and its front is white. Its wings show a white bar at rest and quite prominent white patches on the wings and upper rump while in flight. Its legs are rather short for a shorebird and are flesh-colored with short fat toes. Young birds are brown on the head but their bills are not nearly as red and their backs are mottled.

The American Oystercatcher feeds extensively upon oysters, clams, and mussels. Its flattened bill also makes it adept at taking the insides out of sea cucumbers, starfish, and sea urchins. They are also fond of larger crustaceans such as crabs, crayfish, and shrimp. While they are feeding along the shoreline they will take worms and fish caught in tidal pools left as the tide goes out. Often when feeding, the Oystercatcher will take the prey out of the water and go ashore to finish eating it so that it won't be lost or swim away. Oystercatchers have learned to force mollusks and other potential food into the crevices of rocks to hold them while eating the soft insides.

Nests are made in shallowed-out depressions in sand or gravel along coastal shorelines. Usually the nest is out in the open where little vegetation exists. Nest predation by gulls, raccoons, and feral animals can be quite severe. Nesting may be attempted several times. Two to three lightly-marked olive-colored eggs are laid in the scrape and incubated for about four weeks by both parents. The chicks are able to follow the parents after a short time but will remain dependent upon them for a long time as they learn to use their strangely-shaped bills to open mollusks.

American Oystercatcher

SEMIPALMATED PLOVER *Charadrius semipalmatus*

Plovers are wading birds that vary in size from six or seven inches tall to over a foot tall. They are more compact than sandpipers with short thick necks and bills. The populations of the Semipalmated Plover in the southwest are at a maximum during the migration periods of fall and spring, but it can also be found in good numbers during the winter as well. Since many Plovers migrate early in the season, the Semipalmated Plover may return to the coasts of Texas and California as early as July. The month with the least number of Plovers is June when the breeding birds are nesting in the extreme tundras of North America.

The Semipalmated Plover is a small plover at just over seven inches tall. During the winter, this bird's plumage is less spectacular than during breeding season. The Semipalmated Plover has a brown back with a white belly and front. Its legs are yellow-orange; its winter legs are more yellow than orange. Young birds have almost gray legs. Its short bill is somewhat yellow at the base and the tip is dark. Two characteristics that help identify the Semipalmated Plover are the single band across its lower neck and the facial pattern. Its head is brown with a white forehead patch which extends to make a white eyeline. Its throat is white. A wide brown band goes across its face from the bill and merges with the brown on its head.

The name "Semipalmated" comes from the partial webbing between its toes. The plovers prefer the wet shorelines of both freshwater mud flats and saltwater tidal flats. These birds can be found at the water's edge in the wet sandy areas or even further up away from the wet soils. The plover feeds differently than many of the sandpipers, running in short spurts with its head held erect, a characteristic of many plovers.

The Semipalmated Plover feeds on small insects, worms, and crustaceans found in the sandy shoreline and mud flats. Small mollusks make up a good portion of its diet in wet flats, as well as insects and crustaceans found in the wash line.

The populations of the Semipalmated Plover are recovering from the hunting pressure at the turn of the century, but it is still under increasing pressure due to lack of feeding areas during migration.

Semipalmated Plover

WILSON'S PLOVER, SNOWY PLOVER AND PIPING PLOVER

Charadrius wilsonia / Charadrius alexandrinus / Charadrius melodus

These plovers are small chunky birds that frequent the coastal shorelines of the southwest in the winter. They move rapidly along the water line picking up food bits, starting and stopping quickly as they dart back and forth with the wave action. Unlike many sandpipers, these birds have short stocky bills. All these plovers are small at between six to eight inches. The Snowy Plover is the only plover that breeds in northern Texas, southeastern New Mexico and California, Nevada, and locally in Colorado and Utah.

These birds can sometimes be difficult to distinguish apart. The Snowy Plover and Piping Plover have light-colored backs in both winter and breeding plumage. In the winter, the Piping Plover has no black markings on its face or neck. In breeding plumage, it has a single collar (sometimes broken in front) and a headband from eye-to-eye across its forehead. The legs of the Piping Plover are orange-yellow. The Snowy Plover has black markings on its shoulder, cheek, forehead, and black legs. The Wilson's Plover has a dark back like the Semipalmated Plover. The Wilson's Plover has flesh-colored legs, a white forehead accented by a black band at the top of its head, and a heavy throat band. Its face has dark markings from bill to nape. The female Wilson's Plo-ver are similarly marked but not as dark.

All three of these plovers are declining in their breeding ranges. The Piping Plover has almost become extinct in the Great Lakes region with the increase in recreational uses of coastal lands.

The Snowy Plover nests on beaches, sandy areas, and open duneland. A shallow scrape is made near rocks, driftwood, or vegetation. The nest is quite bare and is lined with small bits of whatever material is available from the surroundings: pebbles, shells, or plant material. Two to three black-marked buff eggs are incubated for four weeks by both sexes. The young are able to follow the adults after they are dry. Both parents protect and feed the young. In five weeks the young birds are able to fly and a second nesting may occur.

Top: Snowy Plover   Middle: Piping Plover
Bottom: Wilson's Plover

KILLDEER *Charadrius vociferus*

Probably the best-known and most common of the plovers, the Killdeer is found over all of the southwest as well as the rest of the United States. Of the "ringed" plovers (that is, having one or more black rings around the neck), it is the largest. The Killdeer breeds throughout the southwest in old fields, agricultural lands, meadows, and pastures. Although considered a shorebird, the Killdeer does not need a shoreline to thrive and does quite well in areas developed by humans. Populations greatly increase during the winter months as migrants from the north flow into the southwest.

Two rings, or black bands, across its chest distinguishes the Killdeer from the Semipalmated Plover and Wilson's Plover, which have only one band. Also, the Killdeer is the larger of the three, being ten to eleven inches tall, although it is a bit slimmer. The Killdeer has a beautiful golden-brown rump that is quite pronounced when in flight. Its wings have white markings similar to the Semipalmated Plover and Wilson's Plover. The Killdeer's tail is proportionately longer than the two smaller plovers. Probably the easiest way to distinguish the Killdeer from the other plovers is by its call: *killdeer killdeer killdeer*, which it gives loudly in flight as well as on the ground. It will also give a loud *dee* or *dee dee dee* call when disturbed.

Nesting occurs in almost any undisturbed open area in agricultural lands as well as suburban areas. A scrape is made where there is a mixture of stones and some vegetation and usually four eggs are laid in the nest. Nesting begins in March and incubation takes about four weeks. The eggs are extremely well-camouflaged, being buff-colored with heavy brown markings. The young are able to follow the parents soon after hatching and remain with both parents for another month.

During incubation and rearing of the young, the adults are extremely protective. The adult Killdeer sometimes feigns injury by calling loudly, stretching out its wing, fanning its tail, and flopping about on the ground to lure a potential predator away. As the predator is drawn further and further away from the nest or chicks, the bird seems to become less and less injured, finally flying away when safety is achieved.

The Killdeer eats a variety of insects but will also take a number of seeds. During the rearing of young, insects are the primary food. In the far north the Killdeer can remain longer into the cold season because it eats seeds, unlike many shorebirds.

Killdeer

BLACK-BELLIED PLOVER *Pluvialis squatarola*

The Black-bellied Plover is the largest plover to winter in the southwest and can be quite abundant, especially on the coasts. Similar to the Semipalmated Plover, the Black-bellied Plover nests in the tundra of Canada and Alaska and spends the winter in the lower coastal states. It will also winter as far south as South America. In the southwest, it is most common from late July until migration is complete in May. Although the bulk of the birds leave by May these birds can still be found in all seasons, although June and July have the least amount. One reason that some birds remain during the summer is that it takes a couple of years for the Black-bellied Plover to reach breeding age.

Typical of the plovers, the Black-bellied Plover has a stocky body with a small neck and small black bill. The plumage in winter is dramatically different than that of the breeding season. In breeding plumage, its belly, face and chest are black and its rump is white. In winter plumage, the colors are an extremely muted gray. Its most identifiable characteristic is seen in flight. Its wings have faint white wing patterns. The "pits" at the underside base of the wings are black in color, which differentiates the Black-bellied Plover from other plovers or the sandpipers.

In the southwest, this bird can be found feeding along coastal beaches as well as inland on the beaches of lakes and rivers. Occasionally the Black-bellied Plover can be found foraging in agricultural fields, especially during migration. The Black-bellied Plover generally feeds on small mollusks and crustaceans. It also probes for and eats whatever insects and microorganisms, including worms, it can find at the wash line. Feeding may be quite competitive and territories will be defended.

One way to tell the Black-bellied Plover from the sandpipers and the Golden Plover is by its call. The Black-bellied Plover gives a three-noted clear whistle with the middle note being slightly lower pitched. This call is given in flight or when it takes off after being frightened. The call can be heard a good distance. Calling occurs more often in flight than while on the ground.

Black-bellied Plover
(Bottom: summer plumage)

RUDDY TURNSTONE *Arenaria interpres*

The Ruddy Turnstone frequents the southwestern coasts mainly in migration but it is also a common winter visitor. In the winter, the Ruddy Turnstone can be found on the coasts of North America and into the southern hemisphere. Few of these birds can be found in the interior of the southwest after migration. Agricultural fields and freshwater areas will be used by these birds in migration, but birds staying the winter seem to prefer the coasts. The breeding grounds of the Ruddy Turnstone are the extreme coastlines of northern Canada, Greenland, and Alaska above the Arctic Circle. It prefers to nest in the tundra areas near the coastline.

The Ruddy Turnstone is a small chunky bird, standing about eight or nine inches tall. The winter plumage of the Ruddy Turnstone is quite different than that of its striking breeding colors. In the winter it is brown above with a darker-brown bib or band across its upper chest with otherwise white underparts and white throat. Its legs are orange-yellow and are paler during the non-breeding season. The bill is rather short and stout at the base. The bill has a gentle upward curvature.

In flight, the black-and-white patterns of the wings and back make these birds unmistakable. The most obvious feature is the oval patch of white on its lower upper back and a black bar across a white tail. During breeding, the brown on its back be-comes a golden-brown and its face and neck become a striking black-and-white. The head has strong black-and-white markings, making the Ruddy Turnstone quite beautiful.

The Ruddy Turnstone gets its name from its rust-colored breeding plumage and because it uses its up-turned bill to deftly turn over shoreline stones and debris to locate the critters hiding beneath including crustaceans, mollusks, worms, insects, and whatever else it may find. It is extremely fond of horseshoe crab eggs and will dig down into the sand to find them. The Ruddy Turnstone is also known for stealing eggs from other birds' nests. It therefore likes to associate its nesting grounds with that of other small seabirds.

This bird is not afraid of humans and many people frequenting the beaches and fishing areas of the southwest in the winter can see the Ruddy Turnstone, even coming quite close to it before it flushes from a rock, deck, or fishing pier.

Ruddy Turnstone
(Top: summer plumage)

LONG-BILLED CURLEW AND WHIMBREL
Numenius americanus / Numenius phaeopus

During the winter months, two extremely striking birds can be seen on the beaches and inland waterways of Texas and California: the Long-billed Curlew and the Whimbrel. Nearly two feet tall, they also attract attention because of their extremely long downcurved bills. The bills are nearly half the length the body in the case of the Whimbrel and longer than that in the Curlew. The Whimbrel nests in northern Alaska and near Hudson Bay in Canada. During the winter it is common on both coasts as well as the Gulf coast. During migration it can be found anywhere there is water and has even been found on golf courses and in city parks.

The Whimbrel is tan to grayish brown with a penciled pattern above and streaks below. Its head has striking tan and brown stripes from its forehead to the back of its head. Its long legs are blue-gray in color as is the Curlew's. In flight, the Whimbrel gives a series of sharp clear whistles: *te te te te te*. The Long-billed Curlew is a bit larger than the Whimbrel and usually is more uniform in color. The Curlew is more tan colored than the Whimbrel but its markings are similar although less distinct. The most obvious way to tell them apart is the lack of head stripes on the Curlew.

The Long-billed Curlew nests in the southwestern New Mexico, California, Nevada, Colorado, and Utah as well as locally in Arizona. It breeds in the grasslands of these states and as far north as southern Canada. During the winter, the Curlew is found primarily on the coasts but may also be seen in cultivated fields, marshes, flooded fields, and pastures.

The Long-billed Curlew feeds mainly on insects found in the mud flats and wet soil of the beaches it frequents, but it also takes anything tasty that may present itself. On the winter coasts, it supplements the insects with crustaceans, mollusks, and other invertebrates. The Curlew feeds by walking determinedly through the grass as if on a mission, surprising, catching, and eating whatever it scares up.

The Curlew builds its nest near a prominent feature as if to use it as a landmark. The nest is a shallow depression lightly lined with grasses. Four mottled olive eggs are laid and incubated for four weeks by both parents. After the young are dried, they will leave the nest to forage with the parents. In about six weeks the young are able to fly and leave the family. The parents, especially the male, are avid defenders of the young but as the young begin to fly the family breaks up.

The populations of both birds have declined over the years, partially due to hunting and more recently due to habitat loss.

Top: Long-billed Curlew
Bottom: Whimbrel

WILLET *Catoptrophorus semipalmatus*

The Willet is a common sight along the salty coasts of the southwest. It is more abundant during the winter when migratory birds move into the southwest from the west and north. The birds can be found in the interior where there are lakes and flooded fields. The Willet nests in the northern prairie states and the eastern United States coastline from Texas to Virginia. It spends the winter in the southern United States and as far south as South America. The Willet seems to be holding its own after being hunted extensively.

The Willet is a tall shorebird, standing nearly eighteen inches tall. When it is feeding the bird is quite plain, being a mottled-gray above with faint scaling on its light-gray underparts. Its legs are long and blue-gray. Its body is rather stocky, unlike the Yellowlegs with which it might be confused. The most striking feature of the Willet is the wing pattern which it shows in flight. When the wings are outstretched, they exhibit two heavy-black bands with a white band between them. This pattern is not seen at all when at rest. These black-and-white markings are quite prominent and no other shorebird of this size has these markings.

The call of the Willet during the breeding season is *pill will willet*. In flight, the call is a *wee wee wee* in rapid succession. The Willet hides its nest on the ground near wet areas in thick grasses or sedges. Nesting begins in the southwest during the month of April and is usually complete by midsummer. One brood is produced per year. Being somewhat colonial, the nests of the Willet can be found grouped together in a favorite area.

The nest is sparingly lined with vegetation in which four brown-marked olive-colored eggs are laid. Incubation takes about four weeks. The chicks are able to follow the parents soon after drying. The young may stay with the adults for over a month before the parents leave for other beaches and mud flats.

Feeding along beaches and mud flats, the Willet takes advantage of whatever food it comes across. It readily takes mollusks, aquatic insects, crustaceans, worms, small fish, and whatever else it can capture in the shallow waters. In flooded farm fields it takes advantage of the numerous insects available, especially grasshoppers and crickets.

Willet
(Bottom: summer plumage)

GREATER YELLOWLEGS *Tringa melanoleuca*

Nesting in the tundra, the Greater Yellowlegs is a common winter resident in the southwest. Some of these long-legged waders appear to remain for the entire year. This wading bird can be found along shorelines of freshwater lakes and marshes as well as in saltwater areas. It can also be found in flooded fields and river backwaters. The Greater Yellowlegs is usually found singly or in small groups during the winter because it defends a winter feeding territory. These birds can be found on the southern coastlines from Virginia to California during the winter months.

The Greater Yellowlegs is a rather tall shorebird standing at about fourteen inches. As its name implies, its most striking feature are its long yellow legs. The bill is long, black, thin, and slightly upturned at the end. The bill can be lighter in color near the head. The Yellowlegs is gray overall, being lighter on the undersides. In flight, its back is dark and its rump is white with slight bars across the tail although the tail still appears white. Its gray back and flanks are checkered. Its cheek is a darker gray and a white eye-line is faintly visible. In winter plumage, they appear lighter overall but as migration begins heavier colors and markings begin to appear.

Lesser Yellowlegs are smaller by about four inches, their bill is shorter and slimmer, and their knee joints are not as thick. Another way to tell the Lesser and Greater Yellowlegs apart is to listen to the call. Although similar, the Greater Yellowleg's calls are grouped in three to five calls, whereas the Lesser Yellowlegs only gives the call one to three times. Also, if the bird is robin-sized it is a Lesser Yellowlegs.

The Greater Yellowlegs feeds by wading through the shallow water of lakes and marshes probing for its food. It takes small minnows, crustaceans, insects, mollusks, and a host of other aquatic organisms. During migration it takes berries and seeds. Occasionally it skims the surface of the water for insects that are emerging or that have been blown into the water. Unlike the plovers, the Yellowlegs do not like to feed out of the water and may even wade in water up to their body. The different body sizes keep the two Yellowlegs from directly competing with each other because they feed at different water depths.

Greater Yellowlegs

LEAST SANDPIPER AND WESTERN SANDPIPER *Calidris minutilla / Calidris mauri*

The coasts of Texas and California as well as many inland shallow waters can be rich with sandpiper species during the winter. These small shorebirds are often called "peeps." These two sandpipers are among the most common in winter and are similar in size and habits. As the name indicates, the Least Sandpiper is the smaller of the two at about six inches, whereas the Western Sandpiper is about seven to eight inches long. Both birds are a mottled-brown above with light-gray to white undersides. In breeding plumage, they are richer in browns above and streaking occurs on their breast and flanks. The Western Sandpiper in breeding plumage has a rusty crown and cheek patch.

Two features help tell them apart. The Western Sandpiper has black legs and feet and a longer heavier black bill that is somewhat downcurved at the tip. The Least Sandpiper has yellow legs and feet with a thin black bill that is shorter but also somewhat downcurved. The bill of the Least Sandpiper appears to be darker. Using the legs to tell them apart may result in identification error as mud sometimes covers the yellow feet of the Least Sandpiper. In the winter, the Least Sandpiper has a collar of slight streaking on the upper flanks whereas the streaking in the Western Sandpiper is less prominent and rarely makes a collar.

In the southwest, these two "peeps" act a little different. The Least Sandpiper is infrequently found on the ocean beaches, preferring inland ponds, rivers, and marshes. On the other hand, the Western Sandpiper prefers the sandy beaches of the coastline and when migration is complete it will be found predominately on the coast. The Least Sandpiper is a more widespread wintering bird.

The Western Sandpiper nests on the very northern coasts of Alaska. It is more commonly a migrant along the west coast but can be found along the Atlantic coast during migration and in the winter. In the eastern United States it is not as common as the Least Sandpiper. Although not declining rapidly, the Western Sandpiper has lost some population, possibly due to beach disturbances by humans.

The Least Sandpiper breeds across the northernmost parts of Alaska and Canada to the Atlantic Ocean. It nests in the tundra bogs and wet meadows. It can be fairly common in migration on any shallow body of water and may accompany a flock of larger shorebirds. Populations are stable, probably because of their ability to use a variety of aquatic habitats.

Top: Least Sandpiper
Bottom: Western Sandpiper

SHORT-BILLED DOWITCHER

Limnodromus griseus

A common shorebird of the fall and spring migration seasons, the Short-billed Dowitcher can be found in the southwest during the winter months as well. It is an infrequent summer visitor but some are usually seen each summer. Populations of these birds are highest during the peaks of migration in April and again in August. The Short-billed Dowitcher usually migrates to South America for the winter but often spends it on the Atlantic, Pacific, and Gulf coasts of the southern United States as well. During the winter they can be found from Virginia to California in increasing numbers the further south you go. In the southwest, they are found on the wet shorelines of lakes, marshes, and the coastline beaches. Occasionally in migration, they will be found in flooded agricultural fields. The Short-billed Dowitcher nests in the tundra and bogs of Canada and Alaska.

In the southwest, both the winter plumage as well as the breeding plumage can be seen. The winter plumage is predominately gray-and-white. Its bottom is a whitish-gray with little markings. The upper part of the bird is brownish-gray to gray during the winter. Its head has a white line above the eye and there is a dark stripe though its eye. Its legs are greenish-gray. Another pronounced feature is its white rump and light-gray tail that makes a wedge part of the way up the back. At about a foot tall, the Short-billed Dowitcher's most recognizable feature is its extremely long bill.

Rarer than the Short-billed Dowitcher is the Long-billed Dowitcher, which is more heavily marked on its breast and has a slightly longer bill. The call of the Short-billed Dowitcher is a rapid three-note flute-like *tu tu tu*, while the Long-billed Dowitcher's call is a loud single call of *keek*.

The long bill of the Dowitchers allow them to probe in the wet sand and mud of the shorelines for aquatic insects, crustaceans, mollusks, and worms. The Short-billed Dowitcher seems to prefer the saltwater beaches. The Dowitchers are good swimmers and may take some organisms from the water surface, but they prefer to probe.

Short-billed Dowitcher
(Bottom: summer plumage)

SANDERLING *Calidris alba*

The Sanderling is probably the most recognized and most often seen of the beach sandpipers. It is a winter resident of the southwest and exhibits different color patterns during the winter than in the summer. Rarely will this bird be found in the southwest during the summer, but occasionally Sanderlings can be seen along the coastal beaches. Nor will the Sanderling generally be found inland and then usually only on the beaches of larger bodies of water.

The Sanderling is fairly common along all the southern coasts but nests in the extreme arctic tundra of Canada and Alaska. This little bird is circumpolar and is found in Europe as well as the United States. The Sanderling is found predominately on beaches where wave action stirs up the sandy margins uncovering insects, tiny shellfish, or sand fleas. During migration, the Sanderling may be found with other shorebirds in almost any wet area. Once a wintering territory has been successfully established, the Sanderling will return year after year.

At about eight inches tall, the Sanderling is predominately light-gray, almost white, with black legs. The underparts of the Sanderling are white. Its bill is relatively short and black. In the winter, the Sanderling exhibits a pronounced black shoulder-patch or stripe. In flight a white wing stripe is shown against a dark wing and its outer tail feathers show white. In breeding plumage, which is rarely seen except for in the summer months, its gray upper parts are replaced with a rich-brown or deep-tan color. Also, its breast becomes rust-colored and its white underparts become a light-buff. Immature birds are similar to the winter adults except they are more buff-colored above and not so gray.

Probably the most identifiable characteristic of these small birds is their feeding behavior. The birds gather in small groups of up to a dozen (but usually less) and follow the waves back and forth. When disturbed from the beach the Sanderling flies out over the water giving a *kip kip kip kip* call. But they return quickly to the water's edge just a short distance away.

In the tundra, the Sanderling nests on the ground in a nest lined with soft grasses and leaves. Usually four brown-speckled olive-colored eggs are laid and incubated for about four weeks depending upon the temperature and weather. Occasionally two clutches are produced. Once the young are hatched they grow rapidly, fledging in about three weeks. The adult Sanderlings protect their young in much the same way as the Killdeer which feigns injury to lure potential danger away.

Sanderling
(Top: winter plumage)

AMERICAN AVOCET AND BLACK-NECKED STILT *Recurvirostra americana / Himantopus mexicanus*

A trip to the coastline of the southern United States will almost always include a sighting of these two striking birds. These slim shorebirds are very graceful waders with extremely long thin bills. Both birds breed in the southwest and the winter populations are augmented by northern migrants.

The American Avocet is about eighteen inches tall with a very pretty rust-colored head and neck. Its body is black-and-white with its wings being black with a white patch. Its legs are long and gray-blue in color. Its long thin bill is curved upward at the end.

The Avocet feeds by walking through shallow water sweeping its bill back and forth to stir up small crustaceans and insects. Occasionally when foraging is good the Avocet will walk along in extremely shallow water picking out morsels by sight. This bird nests in the west from parts of Texas and California north to extreme southern Canada.

The Avocet's nest is usually built near water in loose colonies of other Avocets and Stilts. This makes it possible to spot predators and distract them with feigned injuries. The nest can be a simple depression on the ground or built up to almost a foot. Four or five blotched olive-colored eggs are laid and incubated by both parents for just over three weeks. The young are quickly able to follow the adults who stay with them for protection until their first flight which is at about five weeks. Populations of this pretty bird are stable to possibly increasing as we are no longer are destroying our wetlands.

The Black-necked Stilt is also quite slender, but at only fourteen inches, it is not as tall as the Avocet. It has a jet black back with white underparts. Its long thin bill is black and its face is white with a partial white eye patch. This contrast of black and white make this bird very noticeable. Add to this its bright red legs and you have a Stilt. The red legs also trail quite noticeably during flight. The Black-necked Stilt nests in parts of Texas, Arizona, Nevada, Utah, Colorado, and further north to Montana.

Unlike the sweeping motion the Avocet uses to feed, the Stilt picks small insects and crustaceans from the shallow waters and mud flats it frequents. They nest in mixed colonies on flat ground near water. Some nests are built up, perhaps to avoid flooding in periods of high water. Four or five buff-colored blotched eggs are incubated by both sexes for about three to four weeks. As with the Avocets, the young quickly follow the adults and can fly at five weeks. Populations are increasing as they learn to co-exist with man, making use of manmade waterways and sewage lagoons.

Top: Black-necked Stilt
Bottom: American Avocet

WILSON'S PHALAROPE *Phalaropus tricolor*

Three Phalaropes are found in North America, but only Wilson's Phalarope nests in the United States. It breeds from the Great Lakes and Canada to northern California, Utah, Colorado, and very locally in southern California, Arizona, and Texas. It winters in South America so is most common as a shorebird migrant.

Unlike other shorebirds who forage at the water's edge or in shallow water, Wilson's Phalarope swims in circles in shallow water 'spinning' up food from the bottom. To aid in this curious behavior, the Phalarope has feet that are partially lobed, allowing them to move water easily. Even when out in the ocean or Gulf this spinning can be seen. They eat aquatic insects and small crustaceans. In the fall and during migration they also eat aquatic plant seeds, brine shrimp, and flies.

Wilson's Phalarope has a long thin bill and a white face and chin with a broad black stripe from its bill to the back of its neck. Its crown also has a black stripe which meets the eye-stripe. The sides of its neck and wings change from black into a deep rich brown. The rest of the bird is light-gray. In the winter, the rich browns and distinct facial markings disappear and are replaced with a gray upper body and white lower body. A faint gray eye-stripe is present where the black stripe was during breeding.

The courtship and nesting behavior of this bird is reversed from that of other small birds. The larger more brightly-colored female sings and competes for the male who is less brightly colored. After the eggs are laid the male does the incubating—perhaps the first case for "Mr. Mom" or "women's lib."

Their nest is placed on the ground near water, typically in a shallow depression but occasionally in marsh vegetation. The nest is lined with grass and the site is usually selected by the female. Incubation takes about twenty-three days and the chicks are able to follow the male when they are dry. He protects them and broods them until they are able to fly on their own.

Wilson's Phalarope
Top: Female Bottom: Winter plumage

LAUGHING GULL AND BONAPARTE'S GULL
Larus atricilla / Larus philadelphia

Two black-headed gulls which frequent the southwestern coastlines are the Laughing Gull and Bonaparte's Gull. The main difference between them is that the Laughing Gull nests in Texas and eastward, whereas Bonaparte's Gull is only a winter resident.

In breeding plumage, both of these gulls have an entirely black head. However, the Laughing Gull's bill is red-orange whereas Bonaparte's Gull has a black bill. Also, the Laughing Gull has a dark-gray mantle and Bonaparte's Gull a light-colored mantle. In winter, both gulls lose the black head and only the color of the mantle remains to distinguish them apart. Bonaparte's Gull has a black spot directly behind its eye and the Laughing Gull has what appears to be a smudged area from its eye to the back of its head.

Both gulls are considered to be small- to medium-sized: the Laughing Gull at about sixteen inches and Bonaparte's Gull at about thirteen inches. In flight, Bonaparte's Gull can be identified by the extreme white leading edge of its wing, which is noticeable from great distances. Both of these gulls are common on the Gulf coast although Bonaparte's Gull is found on the Pacific coast as well. Occasionally they will be found inland, but they prefer the coastline. The Laughing Gull has learned to adapt to the handouts of man and can be found inland more frequently than Bonaparte's Gull.

The Laughing Gull gets its name from its call which is a loud raucous *ha ha ha ha*. It nests in Texas and all along the coast north to Cape Cod. Bonaparte's Gull nests in Canada, but winters all along the eastern coast of the United States. The Laughing Gull has become increasingly common and in some areas has become abundant.

Both gulls feed on fish and other marine life. The Laughing Gull is more aggressive and will steal food from other gulls and terns. The Laughing Gull nests in the spring with nesting being nearly complete by the end of June.

Usually three to four dark-olive eggs marked with brown are laid on the ground in a shallow depression. The nest is usually well-hidden by dune vegetation and is lined with grasses, small twigs, and beach debris. The nests can be located in fairly large colonies where added protection is afforded by sheer numbers. The eggs are incubated by both parents for about three weeks. The young are fed partially-digested food while small, but as they grow larger and older they will be able to take whole organisms. They leave the nest at about five weeks of age. As in most gulls, immature birds are hard to distinguish because it may take as long as four years for them to reach their mature breeding plumages.

Laughing Gull
Summer plumage, in flight (top left)
Winter, head (bottom, left)

Bonaparte's Gull
Summer plumage, in flight (top right)
Winter, head (bottom, right)

HERRING GULL AND RING-BILLED GULL

Larus argentatus / Larus delawarensis

The Herring Gull and Ring-billed Gulls frequent most waterways, interior and coastal, of the United States. In the southwest and along the coasts of the southern United States they are winter visitors. They nest in the Great Lakes region or further north and west.

These birds can be a bit difficult to identify when seen individually. Both gulls are relatively large, although the Herring Gull is the larger at two feet compared to under twenty inches for the Ring-billed Gull. Both gulls have gray mantles with black wing tips and yellow bills. However, unlike the Ring-billed Gull, the Herring Gull has a red spot on the lower mandible of its bill which some believe is a "feeding spot" that young Herring Gulls strike at to stimulate regurgitation so they can feed. The Ring-billed Gull has a black ring which completely encircles its bill near the tip. The legs and feet of these two birds are also different. The Herring Gull's feet and legs are flesh- to pink-colored, whereas the Ring-billed Gull's feet and legs are yellow. In the adult plumage of both birds, the head and tail is snow-white. Immature birds of both species are a dull-gray overall and take several years to reach breeding plumage.

Both of these gulls are common and abundant winter residents on the southwest coastlines as well as over much of the coastline of the United States. Arriving in early fall, they remain in Florida as late as May. Some immature birds remain along the coasts during the summer but normally all breeding birds will leave. Traditionally, these gulls were primarily birds of the coastlines but because of their scavenging nature they have adapted well to the world of man and can be found throughout the state wherever there may be a free handout as, for instance, in landfill areas. They have also learned to beg for food and are numerous on public beaches. They even frequent the "Golden Arches" where they get handouts of french fries and Big Macs (hold the pickle)!

In the southwest, during fall through spring, they are the most abundant of all the gulls. Of the two, the Ring-billed Gull is the most likely to be seen in the interior while the larger Herring Gull prefers the coastline. Both of these species seem to be increasing in numbers and seem to be expanding their ranges. This population increase has caused some concern for the smaller seabirds, such as the terns, because the larger gulls prey upon them. The Herring Gull and Ring-billed Gull have been known to take the eggs and chicks of terns and nestlings of many shorebirds.

Herring Gull
Head (middle center)

Ring-billed Gull
In flight (top) Head (left)

FRANKLIN'S GULL *Larus pipixcan*

The third black-headed gull that can be found in the southwest is Franklin's Gull. This gull nests in the northern plains into Canada. A common gull of the prairie, it has been called the "Prairie Dove." In the prairies, it sometimes nests in huge colonies numbering into the thousands. A few sporadic local populations and nesting sites are scattered throughout California, Nevada, and Utah. In the southwest, it is most common in the winter along the Gulf coast of Texas and less common in southern California. Franklin's Gull migrates to South America and is only common in the southwest, especially in Texas, during migration. Fall migration is the heaviest with spring migration being drawn out.

The breeding birds have a black hood similar to that of the Laughing Gull and Bonaparte's Gull. The easiest way to tell them apart is that Franklin's Gull has a pink or reddish tinge to its upper breast and neck. In flight, the primary tips have a white band bordering both sides of the black tips. The rest of the upper wing is gray, whereas in the Laughing Gull the black tips graduate into a dark-gray upper wing. Bonaparte's Gull is relatively lighter in color with extensive white "windows" at its wing tips. In the winter, its head is white with a dark cheek extending to its nape. Of the three, the darkest head in winter is exhibited by Franklin's Gull.

During migration, it will frequent any flooded area including agricultural fields in great numbers. As winter progresses, it will frequent coastlines and estuaries as it continues further south to South America. It wanders over the ground scaring up and catching common prairie insects. In the marshes where it breeds, it will take snails, crustaceans, and aquatic insects. As the season progresses, its diet includes seeds and berries.

In the breeding prairie marshes, its nests are built on a floating mass of vegetation. Three light-tan eggs blotched with brown are laid and incubated by both parents for four weeks. The young are fed insects for about five weeks. Occasionally a parent bird may travel a great distance for food. The young generally leave the nest at five weeks, depending on the availability of food and water conditions, but still are attended by the parents for a short time.

Populations seem to be stable overall but fluctuate locally with water conditions in marshes and loss of habitat. Some new nesting areas have been successful over the last couple of decades.

Franklin's Gull
Left: Summer Right: Winter

GULL-BILLED TERN AND SANDWICH TERN

Sterna nilotica / Sterna sandvicensis

The Gull-billed Tern and Sandwich Terns are both black-capped terns of medium size. The Sandwich Tern is the larger of the two birds at about eighteen inches. Their heads are the feature that distinguishes these birds apart from the other terns. The Sandwich Tern has a black bill with a yellow tip in all plumages. In the breeding plumage, its black cap is crested in the back. The Gull-billed Tern has a solid thick black bill which, as its name implies, is more gull-like than tern-like. In the winter, the Gull-billed Tern's head is almost white with a gray wash over the back part and nape. Both have black feet and show only a small amount of dark on the primary wing feathers when in flight.

Both birds nest in the southwest. The Gull-billed Tern nests both inland and along the coasts, primarily the Gulf coast of Texas, although not in large colonies and with dubious regularity. The Gull-billed Tern is one of the most common inland nesting terns. Its nests are placed on smooth beaches, scrapes, gravel pits, and even abandoned bare fields. The nest is placed on the bare ground and ringed with various objects that are at hand. Two or three buff-colored eggs marked with brown splotches are incubated for just over three weeks. Both parents take care of incubation and the young. Fledging occurs in about five weeks.

The Gull-billed Tern, instead of diving for its food, hovers over it, then swoops down to grab it. The diet of this tern includes insects, small mammals, crustaceans, amphibians, spiders, and occasionally reptiles. The Gull-billed Tern is comfortable in the agricultural areas of the southwest. The Sandwich Tern dives for small fish, but it also eats small crustaceans, shrimp, insects, and small squid.

The Sandwich Tern is limited in its nesting area to the coastal areas of Texas. Development and loss of beach property has contributed to the decline of its nesting areas. Usually two buff-colored eggs with dark-brown markings are laid in a nest on open sandy beaches. Little or no nest preparation is done. Incubation is shared for three to four weeks and both parents take care of the chicks until they leave at about five weeks.

Sandwich Tern chicks, after three or four days, join a crèche with other chicks until they fledge. The parents are able to pick their chick out of all the rest of the chicks in the crèche by its call. The crèche is usually composed of both Sandwich and Royal Tern chicks. These terns will associate with each other as adults and even return to nesting areas together. However, the Sandwich Tern, unlike the Gull-billed Tern, is a coastal bird and is infrequent inland.

Gull-billed Tern
Summer in flight (second from top, right)
Winter, Head (bottom right)

Sandwich Tern
Summer, in flight (top left)
Winter, Head (center bottom left)

FORSTER'S TERN AND COMMON TERN

Sterna forsteri and Sterna hirundo

Both the Common Tern and Forster's Tern are medium-sized, being just fourteen inches or so long. They are primarily winter residents of the southwest as well as fall and spring migrants. Both Forster's Tern and the Common Tern breed in east Texas and along the eastern Texas coast. Some straggling birds may occasionally remain for the summer.

The easiest way to distinguish between these two terns is the pattern of the primary feathers in their wings. The Common Tern's primary feathers are dark-gray, whereas the wings of Forster's Tern are white. Forster's Tern also has a longer and more deeply-forked tail than the Common Tern. In winter plumage, which is most common in the southwest, the Common Tern's black cap changes to a smaller black area from its eye around to the back of its head. The black cap of Forster's Tern changes to a black mask which does not go around to the back of its head. Both of these birds have an orange bill that is usually black-tipped.

The Common Tern is usually found in the offshore waters and is not common inland. In the ocean, it feeds upon small fish which it catches by diving into the water. Forster's Tern can be found along the coasts as well as inland in freshwater areas, although it prefers the coastal waters. The Common Tern is not as abundant during the winter months as most of them migrate further south into Central and South America.

Both of these terns commonly breed in the northern parts of North America: Forster's Tern in the west and the Common Tern in the northern United States and Canada. Both of these birds typically lay three buff-colored eggs with brown blotches which sometimes encircle the egg like a wreath. The Common Tern's nest is just a scrape in the sand that is sometimes lined with a few stones and pebbles. The nest of Forster's Tern is more elaborate and is lined with grasses and aquatic vegetation. Incubation takes just over three weeks. Often the third egg hatched produces a weaker chick that may not survive. The young are able to leave the nest in about three to five weeks.

Both Forster's Tern and the Common Tern feed by diving into the water to catch small fish and other marine organisms. Forster's Tern even captures flying insects over inland waters. Both have learned to adapt to man, taking advantage of handouts from beaches and the wakes of fishing boat. Forster's Tern seems to have adapted more easily to man's presence, possibly because the Common Tern is more comfortable over larger bodies of salt water.

Common Tern
Summer, in flight (top left)
Winter, Head (center bottom left)

Forster's Tern
Summer, in flight (second from top, right)
Winter, Head (bottom right)

ROYAL TERN AND CASPIAN TERN
Sterna maxima / Sterna caspia

Unlike the gulls, the terns are very graceful in flight and appear to be sleeker and more slender. The terns have sharply-pointed bills which they use to capture fish as they dive headfirst into the water. Also, gulls sit on the water whereas the terns are constantly in flight.

The Royal Tern and Caspian Tern are the two largest terns found in the southwest or even North America for that matter. Of the two, the Caspian Tern is the largest, at almost two feet with the Royal Tern around twenty inches. In breeding plumage they are quite handsome birds. Their bodies are predominately white with their heads having a strongly contrasting black cap. The Royal Tern has a yellow-orange bill with a black crest on its head. Its tail is forked to nearly half its length and its wing tips don't show much gray. However, the Caspian Tern has quite a lot of gray at its wing tips. The Caspian Tern has a massive burnt-red bill which frequently has a black tip. Both terns have short black legs and black feet.

Often the Royal and Caspian Terns can be seen resting on sand bars or beaches all pointed in the same direction as if in formation. Although these terns are most common along the coasts, in recent years they have been found along inland lakes and waterways. Since these terns nest in the southwest they can be found here throughout the entire year but winter migrants do increase the populations considerably.

Although these terns breed in the southwest, the breeding populations were almost wiped out during the 1800s. Today there are substantial populations on both the Pacific and Gulf coasts. The total numbers seem to be increasing for both species. Although the colonies of these terns are not as large as others throughout the world, some southwestern colonies may number one thousand.

The Royal Tern and Caspian Tern feed on fish, crustaceans, and other small marine organisms. The terns hover before diving into the water to capture a fish or squid. Although they do steal food from other seabirds, this technique is not a primary food-gathering source.

Both of the Caspian and Royal Terns lay their eggs in nests placed on the ground. They normally lay one buff-colored egg with brown blotches, but may occasionally have two. Incubation is about four weeks. In about three days, the Royal Tern chicks leave their parents and join a group, or crèche, of fledglings that are guarded by a few unrelated adults. The adults find and feed the young in these groups. The group affords protection from predation. The young are able to leave the supervision of adults in five to six weeks.

Royal Tern
Early summer, in flight (top left)
Winter, head (bottom center left)

Caspian Tern
Summer plumage, in flight (top right)
Winter, head (bottom right)

BLACK TERN AND LEAST TERN

Chlidonias niger / Sterna antillarum

Two of the smallest terns to frequent the southwest are the Least Tern and the Black Tern. The Least Tern is the smallest at only nine inches long with a wingspan of eighteen to twenty inches. Besides being smaller, it is easy to identify because of its yellow bill tipped in black and, in the breeding adult, its white forehead in an otherwise black head. Its back is gray and its underbody is white. The winter birds have white to the top of their head with a dark stripe through the eye. Its bill is dark in winter. In flight, the primary feathers are light gray. The Black Tern is similar in winter but its wings are a darker gray.

The Least Tern breeds in loose colonies in the prairie states, the Texas coast, and parts of California. Nesting occurs on beaches and most recently on some pebbled rooftops. Wherever it nests there must be water nearby for it feeds on fish, aquatic insects, and crustaceans. Two to three eggs are incubated by both sexes for about three weeks. When the chicks hatch they leave the nest after a few days and seek a place in the shade out of harm's way. Both parents will bring food to the chicks which grow extremely fast, being able to fly at about three weeks. The family may remain together a few months into migration. The Least Tern migrates to the coastlines of South America. It is absent from the southwest during the winter.

The Black Tern is a bit larger than the Least Tern but only by about an inch. Its charcoal-black body and light-gray wings makes it appear larger as well as its larger wingspan of two feet. In the winter, the Black Tern has a dark spot behind its eye, a dark crown, and its body is white below and all gray above.

The Black Tern frequents freshwater marshes, especially cattail marshes. It nests in the appropriate habitat in the northern United States and Canada. During the winter, it frequents the open seas of the Gulf and the Atlantic and Pacific oceans. In its breeding areas, it eats mainly insects, fish, and other aquatic life. At sea its diet is fish. The only area of the southwest in which the Black Tern nests is in parts of California, northern Nevada, and Colorado.

Its nest is placed upon a mound of vegetation, often an abandoned muskrat house. Four pale-brown blotched eggs are laid and are incubated for three weeks. The young dry quickly and are brooded for a few days after which they seek hiding spots near the nest. In four weeks the chicks can fly but may remain with the parents a bit longer. Near the nest the adults can become very defensive, diving and defecating on intruders. Where the marshlands have been drained, this bird is in serious trouble and populations nationwide have dropped seriously since mid-century. Possible pesticide pollution as well as beach development may be the cause.

Black Tern
Top, In flight: summer
Head: winter

Least Tern
In flight, second from top
Head: winter

111

BLACK SKIMMER *Rynchops niger*

The Black Skimmer is a coastal bird that can be found along all of the coastlines of the southwest, often in the company in terns. Dependent for its food on small fish swimming near the surface it is never far from water. It can be found on larger inland waters and occasionally on flooded fields. In the southwest it breeds in California and Texas near the coasts. Usually it is seen skimming the water, as its name implies, or sitting on sandbars with terns and gulls. It is also quite common along the Gulf coastline to Texas and into Mexico. The Black Skimmer has recently colonized the Salton Sea area and San Diego.

The name "Black Skimmer" comes from the fact that its back is black and it "skims" the water for small fish. This feeding characteristic is enabled by its strange bill, which is long and pointed with the lower mandible nearly a third longer than the upper mandible. The bill is flat vertically which helps it glide through the water. The Black Skimmer catches fish by flying just above the water with its lower bill just cutting the surface. When the Skimmer locates a fish, shrimp,or other aquatic organism by feel, a quick snap of the bill captures it.

The Black Skimmer is quite striking with its black back and crown and white face and bottom. Its bill is bright-red with a black tip and its legs are red as well. Immature and winter birds are not as dark above but still retain the basic color pattern. In flight, its tail has a black streak down the center with white outer feathers.

The Black Skimmer nests on coastal beaches and sandbars. Its nests are placed in shallow scrapes among shells and rocks. Nesting has come under increased pressure with the advance of coastal development and any human disturbance can greatly influence it. However, graveled rooftops have begun to provide an additional area for Black Skimmer nests.

Four or five pale buff-colored eggs marked with dark-brown blotches are laid. The buff-color ranges from green and white to pink. Both sexes incubate the nest but it appears that the male is dominant in this process. The female has the role of protector, vigorously defending the nest and young. The eggs hatch in about three weeks, and three to four weeks are needed for the young to be able to leave the nest. While small, the young are fed regurgitated fish but as they become older they are able to take whole fish. The lower mandible is not longer at hatching and stays the shorter length until the birds have almost reached adult size. Juvenile birds cover themselves with sand in order to protect themselves from predators.

Black Skimmer

WHITE-WINGED DOVE *Zenaida asiatica*

The White-winged Dove is a common summer breeding bird of southern California, most of Arizona, extreme southern Nevada, southern New Mexico, and southern Texas. Although it resembles the Mourning Dove, the White-winged Dove lacks the pointed tail and has bright white wing patches visible in flight. The wing patches are not visible at rest except for a narrow band of white along the lower edge. Adult birds have a red eye that is surrounded by pretty bright-blue skin. The legs are a bright fleshy-red. Nearly the same length (twelve inches) as the Mourning Dove, this bird appears larger because of the length of its tail. The body of the White-winged Dove is a rich creamy-brown and its tail has white tips at the outside corners visible in flight.

In the southwest it is usually migratory but many birds stay through the winter, especially if attracted to feeders. Some birds in migration get a wanderlust and a few have been recorded in the upper midwest in fall. In the spring and early summer this bird is very vocal and its cooing can be heard in any area with a few cactus or trees. The call is a quick throaty *who cooks for you* or *who who who-ah*. In many subdivisions it is s well-known early morning call. In riparian country, it is quite common and has adapted to agricultural lands as well.

As is the case for most doves, the diet of the White-winged Dove is mainly seeds with some berries. In desert areas, it eats the small fruit of the cactus and as a water source takes nectar from cactus flowers, in the process acting as a significant pollinator for the saguaro cactus. After harvesting, flocks of these birds may be seen foraging on the ground in grain fields. They are easily attracted to birdfeeders with millet and milo.

Nesting may occur in small colonies but also individually. Its nest is loosely constructed of small twigs, similar to the Mourning Dove's nest. Often it is so loosely woven that the two white eggs can be seen through the bottom of the nest. The nest may be placed in any small tree, shrub, or cactus between six to twenty feet from the ground. The eggs are incubated for two weeks by both birds and the young are fed a regurgitated partially-digested mixture of seeds called "pigeon milk." This rich mixture allows the young to grow quickly and leave the nest in about two weeks. The young birds are called "squabs" and domestic squabs are considered to be a tender gourmet delicacy. Two, and sometimes three, broods are raised each year.

In the southwest the population is stable or even increasing. The numbers are greatest during the last part of the summer as the year's young augment the population. Migration is usually complete by October and any remaining birds will stay for the winter. Spring migration begins in March.

White-winged Dove

COMMON GROUND DOVE   *Columbina passerina*

The Common Ground Dove is about six inches long, about half the size of the Mourning Dove. The Mourning Dove is quite common throughout the United States but the Common Ground Dove is limited to Florida and the southern coastal states to Texas and parts of Arizona and New Mexico. Northward their range extends into the Carolinas.

The Common Ground Dove is the smallest dove in the United States with a comparatively shorter tail than the rest of the doves. In flight, it can be identified by its bright rust-colored primary wing feathers. The head and chest have scalloped markings which give the bird a scaled effect. The male bird is a little more striking than the uniformly gray female. The underparts of the male have a slight pink tinge and its back is a somewhat darker-brown. Its legs and feet are yellow.

In the southwest, the Common Ground Dove is declining in numbers. It is most common in rural areas and old vacant fields and pastures where it can be seen feeding primarily on seeds, although they also eat berries and insects. After the harvest season, it can be found with other doves foraging in grain fields. As they are sparrow-sized, they can be overlooked when feeding on the ground and can be quite startling when flushed. As they fly their chestnut-colored wings are quite evident.

In the southwest, up to four broods can be raised as the Common Ground Dove nests at almost any time of the year. Two white eggs are laid in a loosely constructed nest of twigs placed in small trees or shrubs. The inner nest contains smaller and finer plant material. Occasionally they will reuse their nest or use that of another bird. Incubation is done by both parents for about two weeks. The young are attended by both parents and fed regurgitated food called "crop milk." The young birds, or "squabs" as they are called when feeding on the crop milk, will be able to leave the nest in just under two weeks. They will follow the parents around for a few days begging for food until they are on their own.

The Common Ground Dove's call is a soft cooing similar to that of the Mourning Dove except it is not as pronounced with a little inflection at the end.

Common Ground Dove

MOURNING DOVE   *Zenaida macroura*

The Mourning Dove is the most common dove or "pigeon" in the United States. Although not striking in appearance, nevertheless this bird is quite handsome. Sometimes called "Pinhead," the Mourning Dove has a small head which is characteristic of the family of pigeons and doves. Its overall color is a soft coffee-brown with black spots on the wings. Its neck is an iridescent pattern of metallic colors. Its head has an elongated black spot below the eye. Its tail is pointed and is longer than that of other doves and pigeons with pronounced white-and-black spots at the end. When flying, its wings make a whispery whistling sound and the flapping is quite loud when startled into flight.

The overall length of the Mourning Dove is about twelve inches. This bird is found throughout the southwest and the populations are greatly increased with migratory birds from the north during the winter. In many states, the Mourning Dove is hunted for sport and meat although some of the northern states do not allow this bird to be hunted as it is quite a popular bird at birdfeeding stations. It is not known whether the name comes from its plaintive call or because the familiar call of *caooh oooh oooh oooh* is so evident during early dawn hours.

Nests are placed in trees or shrubs, usually not more than ten feet above the ground. The nest is constructed of twigs loosely woven into a shallow platform. Occasionally, finer plant material may line the nest. Male birds provide the material for the nest while the female constructs it. Normally two white eggs are laid and incubation is about two weeks. As with the Common Ground Dove, the young are fed crop milk and are able to leave the nest in about two weeks. The Mourning Dove probably receives the award for the most broods produced during a year, sometimes up to six. In the southwest and southeast, the nesting season is all year. In the north, nesting may begin even as the snow is leaving.

The diet of the Mourning Dove is grains and seeds. These pretty birds often feed in flocks on the ground, usually in open areas. During the winter, huge flocks may feed together with the winter migrants. The range of the Mourning Dove seems to be expanding, possibly due to the popularity of birdfeeding stations and new habitats created for birds.

Mourning Dove

INCA DOVE *Columbina inca*

Just a bit larger than the Common Ground Dove at about eight inches long, this dove is one of the prettiest when closely observed. In the southwest, the Inca Dove breeds in southeastern California and the desert country of Arizona, New Mexico, and Texas. In flight, the Inca Dove looks similar to the smaller Ground Dove, but its tail is longer with white tips at the end and sides. Its wings may also show white in them. On the ground, the scaled look extends from its head and chest to the entire body. Its eye is red surrounded by blue skin. The call is repetitive pairs: *cooo coo, cooo coo, cooo coo.*

In the southwest, this bird can be found near farms and in suburbs, city parks, and golf courses. The determining factor seems to be the availability of water. As in most of the doves, the Inca Dove's diet consists mainly of seeds but it will take berries and cactus fruit. This pretty little bird comes readily to birdfeeding stations which may be one reason for the expansion of its range northward.

The nest of the Inca Dove is probably the most versatile and substantial of the doves. It can be located in a variety of locations from shrubs, trees, cactus, and ledges of buildings. The nest is first layered with twigs and then lined with softer plant materials of leaves and grass. The female builds the nest from materials the male brings to her. Two white eggs are incubated by both parents for sixteen days and the young are fed crop milk for another two weeks until they are ready to fly. The young will beg from the parents for a short time after fledging. Up to five broods of young can be raised each year.

Large reproduction numbers and the fact that in the fall the birds may have a wanderlust may account for the expansion of the range northward. Some birds have been seen as far north as Oklahoma, Kansas, and Colorado.

Inca Dove

GREATER ROADRUNNER *Geococcyx californianus*

A member of the cuckoo family, the Greater Roadrunner is the best-known bird of the southwest and is synonymous with Texas, California, Arizona, and New Mexico. The Roadrunner is also found in parts of Nevada, Utah, Colorado, and Oklahoma, as well as extreme southern Kansas. However, unlike the other cuckoos it is mainly a ground bird that prefers to run instead of fly.

The Greater Roadrunner is about two feet long and a dull brown-gray overall with brown streaks. Its underside is lighter and unstreaked. Its tail is extremely long and has white outer tail feathers. When standing still it has the habit of raising its tail, sometimes fanning and slowly lowering it. When running, its tail trails behind or wags back and forth. In breeding plumage, its face is quite colorful with a prominent bright-blue cheek patch with a red trailing edge. The Greater Roadrunner's call is a low series of coos like that of the dove but is much lower and slower.

The Greater Roadrunner is a fast runner enabling it to chase down its favorite food: lizards. It will also take a variety of insects, mice, tarantulas, scorpions, small birds, mammals, and occasionally seeds and berries.

The Greater Roadrunner mates for life and sets up a territory that it defends continuously. Its courtship behavior is intricate and showy. One bird entices the other with a stick. The male drops the stick and runs away from the female with its wings spread and its tail raised or wagging. As he approaches her again, he lowers his wings and tail and wags his tail from side to side. He may bow to her and then repeat the dance.

The Roadrunner's nest is built in a shrub or tree, usually four to eight feet from the ground. A rather large platform of sticks is laid and then lined with soft grasses, weeds, leaves, and feathers. Occasionally snake skins are added to the lining. Four or five white to pale-buff eggs are laid and incubated by both sexes for three weeks, although the male is mostly responsible for the majority of incubation. The young are fed for another three weeks until they are ready to leave. After the young leave the nest, they begin to forage but are still attended by the parents for over a month. As they mature, the young are moved from the parents' territory in order to seek their own territory.

Populations fluctuate with the severity of the winters but seem to be remaining stable overall except for some decline in California.

Greater Roadrunner

GROOVE-BILLED ANI *Crotophaga sulcirostris*

A strange bird, the Groove-billed Ani is found regularly in southwestern Texas. However, because of a tendency to wander, the Groove-billed Ani can also be found in Arizona, New Mexico, Colorado, Utah, and Nevada and even the further north. It is quite common to see them in fallow farmlands, woodlands surrounding agricultural areas, and in parks. It hides and nests in the thick areas of brush adjacent to the open fields where it feeds.

The Groove-billed Ani is all black and about a foot tall. Its two most striking features are the long tail that trails behind almost disjointedly and its large grooved bill. In flight, this bird can be very comical as the tail almost seems to drive the bird. Its black body seems somewhat iridescent in some lights. This large bird appears almost parrot-like but without the hook in its bill. Its bill has longitudinal grooves that can only be seen up close.

The Groove-billed Ani feeds in open fields in flocks mixed with cowbirds and other black birds. It is very sociable both when feeding and roosting. Its diet consists mainly of insects that it scares up as it moves through the vegetation. It also imitates the Cowbird or Cattle Egret, taking insects that are scared up by cattle. Occasionally it will even act like an African Tickbird by taking insects from the backs of cattle. It also eats seeds and fruit.

These birds nest in groups. Three or four pairs of birds build a nest and lay eggs in it. The nest is a big bowl lined with green vegetation. Each female lays three or four eggs in the nest which are incubated by all the birds. After two weeks the eggs hatch and all birds attend the young. After only a week the young are able to crawl from the nest and take food in the branches nearby. After two weeks they begin to fly and can leave the nest, but are still attended by their parents. Sometimes two broods are successfully raised.

Populations of the Groove-billed Ani in the southwest are stable to increasing. Their numbers are greatest after nesting and before fall dispersal. Their numbers are generally determined by available habitat.

Groove-billed Ani

BARN OWL   *Tyto alba*

This owl is the most recognizable owl in the southwest or, for that matter, in the world. It is found on almost every continent. The white facial disc is heart-shaped and it appears almost monkey-like, giving it the name "monkey-faced owl." This owl is quite pale, almost white when seen at night. Seen close up its light breast is spotted with brown to rust-colored spots. Standing at about eighteen inches tall the Barn Owl is a rust-brown above and light-buff below.

Breeding throughout the southwest, this owl is common in the correct habitat. Eastern populations are declining and the Barn Owl is on endangered lists for some northeastern states.

The Barn Owl prefers farmlands, open lands, semi-open lands and fallow fields where it can find small rodents, small birds, and other mammals. It nests mostly in barns and abandoned buildings but may also nest in hollow trees, caves, and cliffs. The female is attended by the male while she incubates up to a dozen eggs. The female starts incubation after the first egg is laid, causing hatching to be spread out. Incubation of the white eggs takes four to almost five weeks. After the hatching begins the female broods the young as the male feeds. The first ones hatched get the majority of the food, so when food is plentiful the entire brood will survive but if hunting is poor the youngest lose out to the older siblings.

Once the chicks are two weeks old both parents will feed and in eight to ten weeks, as the young mature, they will leave the roost. In the southwest, two broods each year are common, but in the north the season is long enough only for one.

At night, the Barn Owl flies ghost-like over the fields. It flies back and forth with wing motions similar to that of a butterfly. The Barn Owl uses its keen sense of hearing to locate small mammals and swoop down to catch them in its strong talons. Its facial disc funnels sounds to its ears which are located behind the facial disc. The Barn Owl's hearing is so good that it can locate and capture mice using sound alone. The Barn Owl has special wing feathers that are fringed at the leading edge which results in a noiseless flight that gives no warning to its unsuspecting prey.

Initially, the release of the Barn Owl in the wild seemed to enjoy some success but on closer examination the releases have had no effect upon local populations. Many states have dropped the release program.

126

Barn Owl

EASTERN AND WESTERN SCREECH-OWL

Otus asio / Otus kennicottii

The Eastern and Western Screech-Owls resemble the Great Horned Owl—except that they reach only about eight inches in height. The Eastern Screech-Owl is found throughout the eastern half of Texas. The Western Screech-Owl can be found from west Texas to the Pacific coast. The habitat requirements of these owls are very diverse. Feeding can occur anywhere there are insects and mice along with some sort of perch. Nesting habitats are in areas where trees and cavities are available and it is for this reason that it is said they may be found "where six trees are together."

In the southwest, the Screech-Owls have three color phases. The most common is brown, but the gray and red phase are not uncommon. In fact, all three of the color phases may exist in one brood. Like the Great Horned Owl, these little owls have "horns" or ear-tuft feathers on their heads and heavily-streaked bodies in all color phases. Their eyes are yellow with black centers.

The call of the Eastern Screech-Owl is quite distinct and unforgettable. There are two types: one a quivering whinny that may stay at the same pitch or may descend and the other a soft trill that also wavers but remains pretty much monotone. Usually the trill is soft, but either call can be soft as well, leading one to believe that the bird may be a good distance away when it may well be directly over-head. The Western Screech-Owl gives a series of short "toots" or whistles that increase in frequency. It will also give a couple of short trills.

Both Screech-Owls can be called with a tape or an easily-learned whistle. They may not come as easily during the day, but at night they will almost always respond readily. Since both Great Horned Owls and Barred Owls eat Screech-Owls, don't be surprised if either of these owls fly up to the tape player looking for a free meal!

In many parts of the country, people are putting up nest boxes for owls. In the southwest, nesting begins in March when four or five white eggs are laid. The nest cavity is usually devoid of lining material except a few feathers and debris from prey. About four weeks are required to incubate the eggs and another four weeks before the young will fledge. Young owls will remain in the same tree or nearby for a week or more begging to be fed by the adults.

The diet of the Screech-Owls is predominately insects but mice are also important to them. During the spring, immature birds of other species become a food source. As the summer progresses, large grasshoppers, katydids, and crickets enter their diet. In some areas, the Screech-Owls have wreaked havoc in the chipmunk and flying squirrel populations.

Eastern Screech-Owl

ELF OWL AND NORTHERN PYGMY-OWL

Micrathene whitneyi / Glaucidium gnoma

As its name indicates, the Elf Owl is the smallest owl in the southwest at just under six inches. It is found mainly in the desert areas of extreme southeast California, Arizona, and the Big Bend area of Texas. It comes into the southwest as a summer resident to nest. This sparrow-sized owl is very vocal and is best identified by its call: a series of slurred chirps, barks, and other repeated songs. Some have likened the calls to laughing chuckle.

The Elf Owl has yellow eyes, an extremely short tail, and no tufts on its head. It is a soft-brown overall with light-buff streaking beneath. Faint wing bars are evident and its eyebrows over the facial disc are white. This owl is active at night and looks like a large moth as it silently takes insects.

The Elf Owl nests in tree cavities but will take advantage of any woodpecker hole. The giant saguaro cactus is a favorite for nesting and roosting. Usually three white eggs are laid and incubated by the female for twenty-four days. The male attends the female during nesting. The female remains with the young while they are small and the male does all the feeding. After two weeks the young are able to eat young insects. The young are able to leave the nest after another two weeks, but they will continue to beg for food for a time.

In most of Arizona, the Elf Owl is holding its own but in some local areas they are decreasing.

The Northern Pygmy-Owl is not much larger than the Elf Owl at about seven inches high. The barred tail of the Pygmy-Owl is longer and is a darker brown. It too is an earless owl, with heavy streaks on its breast. One of its most striking features is the two black spots outlined in white on the back of the head appearing almost like a second set of eyes. Absent in Texas, the Pygmy-Owl can be found in California, Arizona, New Mexico, Colorado, and Utah. This owl prefers wooded canyons and mountains. It also seems to prefer higher elevations. It has adapted to mixed woodlands and open areas. Its call is a soft *too too too too*. The Pygmy-Owl feeds on a large variety of prey including small mammals, birds, insects, and lizards and is a very aggressive hunter. Like the Elf Owl, it is a permanent resident in these states and further northward. This owl can be readily called by tape.

The Pygmy-Owl nests in tree cavities made by woodpeckers. Four white eggs are incubated by the female while the male feeds her. The eggs take four weeks to hatch and the young take another four weeks to fledge. While the young are very small, the female broods them constantly while the male feeds the entire family.

The Pygmy-Owl is probably one of the most widespread of the western small owls and is holding its own.

Top: Elf Owl
Bottom: Northern Pygmy-Owl

BURROWING OWL *Athene cunicularia*

As its name implies, the Burrowing Owl lives in burrows in the ground. It is unique to the southwest and western United States where it is found over much of the prairie land. The populations have decreased significantly due to farming and development. Another reason for the population decline is the elimination of prairie dogs to make burrows. However, the Burrowing Owl has learned to build colonies in vacant lots, golf courses, parks, pastures, airports, and schools. Some communities have taken small colonies 'under their wing,' so to speak, and keep vacant areas out of development for these little owls. The populations of Burrowing Owls are on the comeback and even seem to be expanding northward. During the fall, and occasionally in the spring, vagrants travel from the south and Florida and from as far north as Michigan and Maine.

The Burrowing Owl stands about ten inches tall and seems to be mostly leg. Their overall color is a light chocolate-brown with a mixture of bars and spots. Its face has distinct white-and-black chin markings and it has small white spots on the top of the head. Its eyes are yellow. Immature birds lack the heavy spotting on the breast. It is most often seen standing on small mounds of dirt at the entrance to its burrow, bobbing its head to gain depth perception. Because it looks as if it is bobbing 'hello' it is also called the "Howdy Owl."

Normally found in vacant fields, these little owls can be seen on fence posts, both day and night, surveying the area. Feeding is done predominately at night, but if young are present then they feed in the day as well. When disturbed these little owls will give a series of *clacks* or *chacks*. During the night or dusk hours it also gives a soft cooing similar to the Mourning Dove except it is higher-pitched. When the nest burrow is threatened, the adults imitate a rattlesnake's rattle to discourage would-be predators.

The nest burrow is most often a mammal-made burrow, usually that of a squirrel or prairie dog. Their nest is lined with materials at hand, from cow manure to their own feathers. The burrow extends downward at an angle and is from four to eight feet long with an enlarged nest cavity at the end. In the southwest, five to six eggs are common. The eggs are white but become quite dirty from the nest burrow. Incubation is done mostly by the female and takes three to four weeks with the young fledging in about four weeks. They will remain together as a family for several more months. Nesting is usually complete by mid-summer. Only one brood is raised during a year.

Burrowing Owl

SPOTTED OWL *Strix occidentalis*

Probably no owl has had so much notoriety and fame as the Spotted Owl. In the southwest, the Spotted Owl can be found in the right habitat in California, Arizona, New Mexico, Utah, and a small portion of Texas. From California it is found northward along the coast to Oregon, Washington, and British Columbia. The northern population is the one in extreme jeopardy because of the removal of old growth forests. In the southwest, it can be found in wooded canyons and mature mountain forests.

The Spotted Owl is a medium-sized owl closely resembling the Barred Owl. As the name indicates, the Spotted Owl has spots on its entire body, whereas the Barred Owl has bars across its neck and streaks on its breast. Both have dark-brown eyes and yellow bills. At nearly twenty inches tall, the Spotted Owl is a rich soft-brown overall, with no ear tufts. As in most of the large owls, the female is larger than the male.

The call is the easiest way to tell the Spotted Owl from the Barred Owl. The Spotted Owl gives a series of loud hoots with a hesitation before the last call.

A nocturnal feeder, the Spotted Owl feeds mainly on small woodland mammals. It will take some birds, large insects, and lizards. Since bats are quite plentiful in parts of the southwest they are sometimes taken by Spotted Owls as well. Using its keen sight, the Spotted Owl hunts from a perch and swoops down to capture its prey.

Nesting is usually done in a well-protected territory. The Spotted Owl can be induced to come close by playing a tape of its call and can be approached closely while on its roost. It is very territorial and will come to defend the area, allowing a close view. Some feel the birds pair for life and will remain in the same defended territory for years. Breeding may not occur each year. Be careful not to overdo the tape playing, especially during breeding season.

The nest is usually in a hollow tree, cliff, or old hawk's nest. Very little is done to the nest, which is generally just a hollowed-out area. Two or three white eggs are incubated by the female for about four weeks. The male attends the female during incubation. The early young are brooded by the female for a couple of weeks before she joins the male to supply food for the hungry young. In another three weeks the young will be able to leave the nest.

Young owls have a difficult time learning to hunt efficiently and a good percentage will not make it to their first nesting season.Those that do may live for a long time. The Spotted Owl is losing ground in the northwest, partially due to loss of the old growth forests to logging and possibly due to the takeover of the more aggressive Barred Owl. In the southwest it seems to be stable.

Spotted Owl

COMMON NIGHTHAWK AND PAURAQUE

Chordeiles minor / Nyctidromus albicollis

Probably the most recognized member of the Nighthawks is the Common Nighthawk. Its wings are pointed like a hawk's and since it flies at night what better name to give it than 'Nighthawk'? In the southwest it is a summer resident where it nests. It arrives during March and nests by April. By late September it has left for the South America. This bird prefers semi-open areas: pastures, agricultural fields, and grasslands. It has also adapted to urban areas, especially lakes and waterways.

The Common Nighthawk makes a loud harsh *peeent* as it feeds as well as a loud *boom* when the male dives downward to attract the female. In flight, a pronounced white bar is evident across the primary feathers of the wing of the Common Nighthawk and its throat exhibits a white patch. Its wings are long and pointed and its tail is long with a slight notch. Male birds also show a white band across the end of the notched tail. The overall color is a brown-gray with camouflage markings. This color combination makes the Nighthawk almost impossible to see on the ground where it roosts and nests.

Although it feeds mainly at night, the Common Nighthawk can be seen during the day. It is a common night visitor at shopping malls where it can be seen diving around the street and parking lights where insects gather. It is also found near waterways where dobsonflies and mayflies are found.

The Common Nighthawk dives after insects and captures them in its huge gaping mouth which is lined with stiff bristles.

Nesting normally occurs on the ground, usually in well-drained open areas but it has also learned to place its nest on the flat gravel roofs. No real nest is made; at the most a slight depression is used. Its eggs are heavily camouflaged in earth tones with a fine mottling that makes them appear like the leaves or the stones upon which they are resting. Two eggs are laid and incubated for two to three weeks. The young are fed regurgitated insects and fledge in about three weeks. The young birds are lighter in color than adults. As September arrives most of the birds migrate south although a few stragglers may remain as late as November.

The Pauraque is related to the Common Nighthawk, but is found only in the southeastern part of Texas. Its habits are similar to the Common Nighthawk. Identification of the Pauraque is easy because its tail is rounded and long. The call is a distinctive descending *purr* or *whirr* given while in flight or on the ground. The Pauraque is found only in Texas. It can readily be seen in the correct habitat by traveling the roads at night and listening and watching for its shining eyes which can be seen a good distance away. The Pauraque can be found in parks along the Rio Grande in all seasons.

Common Nighthawk

CHUCK-WILL'S-WIDOW   *Caprimulgus carolinensis*

The Chuck-will's-widow and Common Nighthawk belong to the family of birds called the 'Nightjars' or 'Goatsuckers.' They are characterized by extremely large gapes (two inches for the Chuck-will's-widow) with which they capture insects in mid-air in their small soft bills.

At nearly twelve inches long, the Chuck-will's-widow is the largest of the Nightjars. It is a well-camouflaged soft-brown overall. In flight, both its wings and tail are rounded at the tips. The tail of the Chuck-will's-widow is longer than the Nighthawk's. Its throat is buff-colored with a white stripe below which sets off its dark breast. A closer look will reveal that the male has white in its outer tail feathers which are lacking in the female.

Location and voice are the best way to identify these birds. As its name implies, the call of the Chuck-will's-widow is a sharp and loud *chuck-will's-widow*. Unless you are relatively close the *chuck* can be difficult to hear. They call during the evening, morning, and night hours either in flight, when sitting on the resting perch it uses to sleep on during the day, or from seldom-used roadways. A good place to see and hear these birds is in the Texas state parks. In the southwest, the Chuck-will's-widow is found only in Texas and eastward. If you drive slowly, you can hear them calling and may see their tell-tale red eyes in the glow of the headlights. During the day, the Chuck-will's-widow sleeps on the ground or a horizontal branch or fence rail, leaving its resting place to feed at night. Often it will return to the same roost day after day and even year after year.

In Texas, the Chuck-will's-widow is a year-round resident. It is predominately an eastern bird, ranging from the Texas coast to the mid-Atlantic states and north to the southern Great Lakes. But only Texas, Louisiana, and Florida have these birds the entire year. Even so, most will leave to winter in South and Central America.

The nests are made in a slight depression in the leaves of the forest floor in April. Two well-camouflaged eggs are incubated by the female for about three weeks. The young are able to help themselves soon after hatching and can hide themselves. The female takes care of the young for about two to three weeks before they are able to leave. Only one brood is produced a year.

The diet of the Chuck-will's-widow is predominately insects, especially large beetles and moths. The large gape (mouth) is lined around the edge with long stiff bristles to help guide insects into its mouth. It has been known to take small birds while in flight, swallowing them whole. Like owls, the flight of these birds is quite silent.

138

Chuck-will's-widow

CHIMNEY SWIFT *Chaetura pelagica*

In the southwest, the Chimney Swift is found in most of Texas and the eastern portion of New Mexico; further west it is replaced by the White-throated Swift. This bird is a small, dark, and fast-flying. They can be seen during the day flying high in the sky hunting insects. Their wings are pointed and their body is short and cigar-shaped, so much so that the Chimney Swift has been called the 'Flying Cigar.'

The Chimney Swift appears almost to have no tail with the portion of its body in front of its wings almost equal to that behind its wings. Its underside is a little lighter but it is not noticeable except upon close viewing. The White-throated Swift has a white throat and belly with dark side patches. Its tail is unforked. In flight, the Chimney Swift gives off a constant chattering especially when approaching the nesting chimney.

In Texas and New Mexico, this bird is a common migrant and summer resident. It arrives from South America during March and begins nesting in April. It commonly nests in hollow trees, caves, caverns, chimneys, and wells. A crescent-shaped nest is built of twigs which are glued together and attached with powerful saliva to the inner side of the chimney wall. It may take a month for the nest to be completed, and even then it doesn't appear very substantial.

Four to five white eggs are laid on the small platform and incubated by both parents for about three weeks. Usually the nest is placed a good distance down the chimney, almost to the bottom on a residential home chimney, and twenty feet or more into commercial chimneys. Often nesting is communal and additional non-breeding birds may assist in the incubation and care of young. The young remain in the nest for up to a month, becoming quite loud during the last couple of weeks. Prior to leaving the chimney the young are able to crawl about with sharp claws. If the temperature gets too hot in the chimney, the adult birds hover over the nest, fanning the young. They can keep this up for fairly long periods. Post-breeding populations can produce quite large flocks that roost together in some of the larger chimneys. By the end of October, the Chimney Swift has left the southwest for South America.

The Chimney Swifts are related to the Hummingbirds in that they have very small feet and short legs. Their wing beats are very rapid and they almost never land on any flat horizontal surface. The Chimney Swift's feet are very short and most of their time is spent in the air. Some people have even said that they don't ever land.

Chimney Swift

BROAD-BILLED AND BLACK-CHINNED HUMMINGBIRDS

Cynanthus latirostris / Archilochus alexandri

The southwest is blessed with the largest number of hummingbirds in the United States and occasional rarities even show up from Mexico. The Broad-billed Hummingbird is only found in the southwest part of Arizona during the breeding season. It prefers wooded and desert canyons at fairly high elevations of about five thousand feet. Occasionally this bird will show up in California and Texas.

The Broad-billed Hummingbird is one of the smaller hummingbirds at around four inches in length. The adult male is a dark iridescent green with a blue throat or "gorget." Its bill is red-orange with an occasional black tip. The female is a dull-green above and gray below and may exhibit a white eye-stripe. Its tail is short and squared off at the end.

The nest is placed in a fork of a branch of a deciduous tree. The tiny cup-like nest is usually placed from eye level to about ten feet above the ground. It is constructed of grasses and spider webs and lined with plant down. As is the case with many hummingbirds, the female builds the nest and camouflages it with bits of bark and dead leaves, making it look like a knot on the branch. Two white eggs are incubated by the female for about two weeks. The young are attended by the female until they are able to fly. The brooding period may vary from two weeks to nearly a month

depending upon the weather and the availability of food. A second nesting may occur at the end of July, the rainy season. A few birds will stray and remain for the winter.

The Black-chinned Hummingbird is also very small at a little over three inches. It is found in most of the southwest in the summer. Its chin is black with a violet border beneath and a pronounced white border beneath that. As with most hummingbirds, the iridescence can be seen only in the right reflective light. This hummingbird is green above and white beneath with gray-green flanks.

The female builds the nest on the horizontal branch of a tree or shrub between five and ten feet off the ground. The nest is constructed of soft plant fibers held together with spider web, lined with plant down, and camouflaged with dead leaves and plant bits. Two white eggs are incubated by the female and hatch in about two weeks. The young are the sole responsibility of the female and she will feed them for about three weeks; on rare occasions for four weeks. If the season is good, the female may begin building a nest for an additional two or three hatches.

This little hummingbird is easy to attract to a feeder using sugar water. It rarely overwinters north of Mexico. A few birds, probably juveniles, will stray eastward as far as Louisiana.

Top:
Black-chinned Hummingbird
Left: Male. Right: Female

Bottom:
Broad-billed Hummingbird
Left: Male. Right: Female

BLUE-THROATED HUMMINGBIRD

Lampornis clemenciae

Among the largest of the hummingbirds found in the United States is the Blue-throated Hummingbird. It is nearly six inches long and when seen alongside the Black-chinned or Rufous Hummingbird it appears massive. This hummingbird is dark-green above and gray below. The male has a large blue throat. Its tail is large and black with the tips showing large white spots. Its eye has a prominent white stripe and its cheek is black or dark-gray. The female is lacks the blue throat and is a bit lighter in color overall. The Blue-throated Hummingbird can be found in Arizona and Texas, usually in canyons where water can be found. It is a frequent user of hummingbird feeders in the correct habitat. It does not require the higher elevation of some of the other Hummingbirds.

A summer resident, the Blue-throated Hummingbird feeds on the nectar of most flowers but seems to be attracted more often to orange or red flowers. It will take many of the insects associated with the flowers as well as spiders, especially during nesting and in seasons with few flowers. During the lean times, feeders are very important. At feeders, the Blue-throated Hummingbird can be very aggressive, driving away other hummingbirds and even orioles trying to feed. Their call is a loud *seet* which is repeated often when they are excited.

The male's role is mainly that of attracting the female with his ritual flights in which he spreads his large tail and shows the bright white spots. He defends the territory for the female but that is the extent of "duties." The female makes a small cup-like nest of soft grasses and plant fibers. The interior is lined with plant down and moss. The outside is also camouflaged with moss held together with spider webs. The Blue-throated Hummingbird has the greatest variety of nest sites. It usually nests in trees or shrubs from just a couple of feet to over thirty feet above the ground. It prefers thick branches but has also been known to nest in caves, ledges, tree trunks, and human structures. It is a real treat when this large hummingbird nests on an eaves, ledge, or corner of a porch.

The female incubates the two white eggs for about eighteen days and feeds the young for another four weeks by pushing her long bill down their throats and regurgitating a mixture of nectar and animal material. While she is feeding her young, the female needs more spiders and insects for protein.

In Arizona and Texas, the Blue-throated Hummingbird is holding its own and the summer populations may be increasing where feeders are present. In Mexico, the populations may be declining because of loss of habitat. During fall migration these bird may wander throughout the United States, although these are probably juveniles.

Blue-throated Hummingbird
Top: Male   Bottom: Female

BROAD-TAILED AND RUFOUS HUMMINGBIRD

Selasphorus platycercus / Selasphorus rufus

The Broad-tailed Hummingbird breeds over much of the southwest with the exception of the coastal areas of California and the eastern part of Texas. In these areas it breeds primarily in the mountains where it prefers semi-open woodlands and meadows with an abundance of wildflowers. During migration it can be found over most of the southwest.

At about four inches in length, this little hummingbird reminds many people of the Ruby-throated Hummingbird. Both sexes of the Broad-tailed Hummingbird are metallic-green above and white beneath. The female's throat is speckled and she may show a buff-color on her flanks. The male has a bright-red gorget. The most reliable means of identification is by the shrill metallic trilling sound made by its wings which can be heard a good distance away. These birds are very territorial about their feeding areas and will defend a patch of wildflowers from other hummingbirds.

Breeding begins with the male defending a territory by flying high up in the air and diving, accentuating the wing noises. The female builds the well-camouflaged nest on a horizontal branch. The nest is constructed of soft plant material held together with spider webs and lined with plant down. The outer part of the nest is camouflaged with lichens and mosses. Two white eggs are incubated by the female for two to three weeks. The chicks are fed by the mother for about four weeks, depending on the availability of food. As the young grow, the nest flexes and expands to accommodate them, who usually end up outweighing the female at fledging. The Broad-tailed Hummingbird winters in Mexico although recently some have remained later than normal at feeders, probably stragglers from the northern part of the United States.

The Rufous Hummingbird is found in the southwest only during migration. However, increasing numbers are overwintering and are showing up at feeders more frequently. It nests in the northwestern part of the United States and Canada up to and including Alaska. This little hummingbird is similar to the rare Allen's Hummingbird, having rust-colored sides, belly, tail, and back. The tail of the female is predominately green with some rust. The male has a bright orange-red gorget but the female also has red spots on her throat.

This little bird breeds the furthest north of all the hummingbirds and also has quite a wanderlust during fall migration. It has shown up at feeders in the east as late as mid-December. At night it finds a secluded spot and goes into a state of semi-hibernation called "torpor" in which its body temperature and metabolism drop to conserve energy and survive the night.

146

Top:
Rufous Hummingbird
Left: Male Right: Female

Bottom:
Broad-tailed Hummingbird
Left: Male Right: Female

MAGNIFICENT AND VIOLET-CROWNED HUMMINGBIRD

Eugenes fulgens / Amazilia violiceps

The Magnificent Hummingbird only breeds in southeastern Arizona and southwestern New Mexico but migratory birds can show up all over the southwest. This hummingbird is green above and dark on its belly, the female being a bit lighter than the male. The male has a bright-green throat, purple crown, and fairly deeply-notched tail.The female's tail is more squared-off with white outer tail spots. Both sexes have white spots behind their eyes, the female's being less prominent.

These birds prefer forest in the canyons and hillsides of the higher mountains.In its range, it is a common summer resident and populations seem to be stable. The Magnificent Hummingbird nests in coniferous and deciduous forests. The female selects a nest site between fifteen and forty feet above the ground (sometimes higher) and builds the nest of soft plant fibers, plant down, and spider webs.The outside is plastered with lichens and bits of bark. Two white eggs are incubated by the female for sixteen days and she attends them until they are ready to fledge at about three weeks. She feeds the young a mixture of nectar and insects that is partially digested. She will take insects from the air as well as glean them from leaves and tree bark. The Magnificent Hummingbird has been seen removing captured insects from spider webs.

Breeding in almost the same territory as the Magnificent Hummingbird is the Violet-crowned Hummingbird. The male has a bright-violet crown. The underparts of both sexes are white and their backs are a metallic green. Its bill is rather long and is orange-red with a black tip.

This bird prefers lower elevations along streams. It seems to prefer canyons with sycamores, cottonwoods, and other deciduous trees. It is not totally dependent on flowers for a food source and is quite adept at foraging for insects among the shrubs and trees along streams.

The female builds a nest, preferably in a sycamore tree, on a horizontal branch about fifteen to twenty feet above the ground. She builds the nest from soft plant fibers and lines it with down from cottonwood and willows. It is held together with spider webs and camouflaged with lichens, bark bits, and small twigs. The two white eggs take about two weeks to hatch and the female is solely responsible for incubation and rearing of the young.

The Violet-crowned Hummingbird population seems to be increasing in the southwest and may even remain over the winter where feeders and food are available. Other than Mexico, Arizona, and the extreme southwest, New Mexico is the best place to see this bird.

Top:
Magnificent Hummingbird
Left: Male Right: Female

Bottom:
Violet-crowned Hummingbird
Left: Male Right: Female

COSTA'S AND ANNA'S HUMMINGBIRD

Calypte costae / Calypte anna

Costa's Hummingbird is a small bird found predominately in the arid desert regions of California, Arizona, and a small part of Nevada. The male Costa's Hummingbird has a dark-violet crown, face, and throat. Its gorget extends out and downward from its throat like a long handlebar mustache making it highly identifiable from a great distance. The gorget and crown separate behind the eye, giving the male a white triangle behind the eye. The female is green above and white below.

To avoid the hot summer, nesting begins in late winter and early spring. The female builds the nest in yuccas, agaves, cacti, or other desert shrubs. The nest is usually located close to the ground and in the open. It is loosely constructed of soft plant fibers, leaves, grass, and bits of leaves and flowers held together with spider webs. The two white eggs are incubated by the female for two to three weeks. The young are able to leave the nest in another three weeks. The male is quite vocal during courtship, flying down in front of her and giving off loud squeaks. After mating, he departs and pairs up with other females.

Costa's Hummingbird is common during the season and may overwinter. Populations are stable and adaptation to suburbia seems to be occurring in desert areas.

Anna's Hummingbird is one of the few permanent residents of the southwest. It can be found in Arizona, California, and along the Pacific coast into British Columbia. It prefers open scrubby areas but can also be found in city parks and suburban backyards. As in many of the hummingbirds, Anna's Hummingbird seems to like stream sides where there are more insects, flowers, and nesting materials.

The male is about four inches in length and has a bright rose-red head, face, and neck. Its lower parts are gray graduating into green to the tail. Its back is green. The female has red spots on her throat but lacks the overall bright-red color. The male is more vocal than most hummingbirds. He makes squeaks, pips and grating noises, especially in the diving U-shaped flight he uses to attract a female.

As a permanent resident, Anna's Hummingbird may begin nesting around the first of the year. Its nest is built on a flat surface or branch. A small cup is made from plant fibers and lined with plant down and feathers. The exterior is camouflaged with lichens and the whole thing is held together with spider webs. After mating, the female incubates and rears the fledglings. The eggs take about two to three weeks to hatch and the young leave the nest in another three weeks. After nesting, migration occurs east and west but the population as a whole remains relatively stable. Anna's Hummingbird has adapted to nesting on decks and porches.

Top: Costa's Hummingbird
Left: Female Right: Male

Bottom: Anna's Hummingbird
Left: Male Right: Female

ACORN WOODPECKER *Melanerpes formicivorus*

The Acorn Woodpecker is probably one of the most striking and colorful of the southwestern woodpeckers. In flight, its black body is accented by a large white rump and white patches in the wings. Its head is striking with black surrounding its eye, a white cheek and neck, and red crown. The head of the male is red with no black in front; the pattern from the top of its bill is black, white, and red in that order. The female's head is red interrupted with black; the pattern is black, white, black, and red in that order. The Acorn Woodpecker is similar in size to the Red-headed Woodpecker at about nine inches tall. In the southwest, it can be found in California, Arizona, New Mexico, and parts of west Texas. Except for California, its northern range is within these states. On the Pacific coast it reaches up into Oregon. In this part of the United States it is a permanent resident.

The Acorn Woodpecker is found in oak forests but also in open forests of other deciduous trees as well as mixed conifers. The most common habitat is mixed deciduous forests with a variety of oak species to guarantee some acorns for winter eating.

The Acorn Woodpecker is a communal bird, forming small colonies as well as nesting in common nests. The birds are best known for hoarding acorns for the winter. They may drill as many as 50,000 round holes into snags, dead trees, and buildings to store the acorns! The diet of the Acorn Woodpecker is predominately acorns. It will also eat other seeds, insects, and berries, but rarely excavates trees to locate insects.

Colonies of nesting Acorn Woodpeckers are usually made up of a few breeding males and about three breeding females. The entire group defends the nest site and the food cache, or "granary tree." Five to fifteen eggs are laid by the various females. Normally only the breeding birds incubate, but occasionally the non-breeding adults may help, changing with their nest partners a couple of times per hour. The white eggs hatch in about two weeks and everyone helps feed the young birds. The young woodpeckers will be able to leave in about four weeks. The colony may nest as often as three times each year.

The population of Acorn Woodpecker seems to be stable and is common where the habitat is correct.

Acorn Woodpecker

NORTHERN FLICKER   *Colaptes auratus*

The Northern Flicker is also called the Gilded Flicker and is the only woodpecker that commonly feeds on the ground on ants and other insects. Three types of flickers have been combined to become the Northern Flicker: the Yellow-shafted, Red-shafted, and the Gilded Flicker. The Gilded Flicker is the one that breeds in the southwest and intermediate forms can be found as eastern populations intermingle.

The Northern Flicker is a large woodpecker at over twelve inches in length. The back of the Northern Flicker is brown with heavy black bars and its underside is light-buff with dark spots. Its most conspicuous identifying features are its white rump patch and its bright-yellow underwings, both seen in flight. Its cap is a light-gray and the back of its nape is red. The lower part of its neck sports a black crescent which separates its spotted breast from its unspotted throat. The male has a black stripe rising from the base of the beak going back across the cheek, commonly called a "mustache." Its call is a loud *flicka flicka flicka* or *wic wic wic wic,* or sometimes a single note: *kleep.*

In most of the southwest, the Northern Flicker is a permanent resident. It is common in parks and open woodland areas and has adapted quite well to suburbia where it can find trees in which to nest. During the winter many migrating Northern Flickers invade the southwest. The Northern Flicker can be something of a nuisance as well because they drum on buildings to attract a mate or to get at insects. The afflicted homeowner can usually scare them away with persistence.

The Northern Flicker nests in tree cavities although many people are having success with them in nest boxes. Nesting may occur as early as March and a second brood may be produced by late spring. Generally five to eight white eggs are laid and both parents incubate them for about two weeks. The young are fed regurgitated food for about four weeks at which time they are able to fledge. Successful nest cavities are used repeatedly year after year. Two broods are more common in the southwestern states than in the northern states.

Northern Flicker

Hairy Woodpecker and Downy Woodpecker

Picoides villosus and Picoides pubescens

The Hairy Woodpecker and Downy Woodpecker are very much alike, except for size. Of the two, the Downy Woodpecker is the more common. Both are permanent, widespread residents in Florida, although the populations of Hairy Woodpecker are declining due to the loss of trees.

The backs of both woodpeckers are black and their wings black with white spots and markings. The front is also white. The head has a black cheek patch with white markings above and below outlining the black patch. The white may reach around to the back on some birds. The males of both species have red patches on the back of the head, sometimes meeting the white. The bill of the nine-inch Hairy Woodpecker is about twice the width of the head. The six-inch Downy Woodpecker has a short bill, about half the width of the head. Both birds have black center feathers and white outer tail feathers. The Downy Woodpecker may show some black markings on the outer white tail feathers. Both birds give a whinny call and a solitary *peek*; with the Hairy Woodpecker's call being more slurred and lower-pitched.

These two birds are tree cavity nesters and are limited in range partly because of lack of suitable nest cavities. Most often they excavate their own nest cavities, but they will sometimes they will take over existing holes. One difference between them is that the female Downy Woodpecker usually selects the nest site, whereas the male Hairy Woodpecker usually selects its site. In both cases both sexes will incubate and brood the young. Incubation for both species lasts about two weeks; a day or so longer in the Hairy Woodpecker's case.

The young are fed a diet of regurgitated insects and will leave the nest in about four weeks. The young may accompany the adults for a few weeks after fledging. For the Downy Woodpecker in the northern part of the United States, one brood is most common—in Florida, two broods are possible. The Hairy Woodpecker rarely has more than one brood even in the south.

The Downy Woodpecker is the most common woodpecker to come to birdfeeders throughout the United States. In the winter it will eat suet as well as sunflower seeds. The normal diet of these woodpeckers is predominately insects but they will take seeds and berries, especially during the fall and winter. A suet/peanut butter mixture seems to be a favorite of both these woodpeckers.

Although they will use nest boxes for roosting in winter, it is rare that these birds will actually nest in a man-made box. Of the two it is more likely that the Hairy Woodpecker will use a nest box, possibly due to the lack of natural nest cavities.

Hairy Woodpecker (left) and Downy Woodpecker (right)

GOLDEN-FRONTED AND LADDER-BACKED WOODPECKER   *Melanerpes aurifrons / Picoides scalaris*

Found only in Texas and a small part of Oklahoma, the Golden-fronted Woodpecker is the southwestern counterpart to the eastern Red-bellied Woodpecker. The male Golden-fronted Woodpecker's head is a cream color overall with a small yellow patch on the top of its bill, a clear forehead, red top, and yellow nape. The female lacks the red top on her head. Her chest and belly is buff and her back is a heavily-barred black-and-white. Her rump is white and faint. White wing patches and a dark tail are visible in flight. The Golden-fronted Woodpecker is absent in the extreme western and northeastern parts of Texas.

The Golden-fronted Woodpecker's preferred habitat is dry forests and brushlands. It is also fond of stream side woodlands where it often nests. Its diet is mainly insects taken from leaves and bark of trees but it will also take seeds, berries, and nuts. It will occasionally feed on the ground like the Northern Flicker. It has adapted well to birdfeeders and human plantings.

As in all the woodpeckers, the Golden-fronted Woodpecker nests in a cavity in a tree, pole, or fence post. Usually the nest cavity is about a dozen feet above the ground but they have been known to nest as close to the ground as a couple of feet. The five white eggs are incubated by both sexes for two weeks and the young are fed for another four weeks. Two broods are usually raised and occasionally a third. The population is stable and the Golden-fronted Woodpecker is a permanent resident in the southwest.

The Ladder-backed Woodpecker is found throughout the entire southern part of the southwest although they also breed in small areas of Nevada, Utah, and Oklahoma.

The Ladder-back Woodpecker has black-and-white bars on its upper body, hence its name. Its underside is buff with black or brown specks. The face of both sexes has a heavy black line which goes through the eye, turns downward, and returns to the base of the bill, making a triangle effect. The male has a red crown, the female a black one.

This bird prefers dry areas of mesquite and shrubs. It can also be found along stream sides and in open groves of woods where it feeds upon a variety of insects and berries. The male is larger than the female and has a longer bill. When they forage together, the male probes the larger branches and trunks of trees while the female feeds on the outer smaller branches.

The nest cavity is excavated and attended by both sexes who pair for the year. Four white eggs are normally laid and incubated for about two weeks. The young fledge in three to four weeks.

This bird is a permanent resident in the southwest in the correct habitat and populations seem to be stabilized.

Left: Ladder-backed Woodpecker (male)

Right: Golden-fronted Woodpecker (male)

PILEATED WOODPECKER *Dryocopus pileatus*

In the southwest, the Pileated Woodpecker is found only in the eastern part of Texas and the northern wooded parts of California. Although it is normally found in large wooded areas and not urban areas it is becoming more common in the southwest as it adapts to wood lots and other urban habitats. Probably the best place to find the Pileated Woodpecker is in manmade parks and preserves where this shy bird can be readily seen and approached.

In addition to its large size, this woodpecker is easy to identify by its flaming-red crest. The cartoon character, Woody Woodpecker, is probably modeled after the Pileated Woodpecker. Both sexes have the crests, but the female's forehead is black instead of red. The faces of both are patterned with black-and-white markings, but the male has a red bar extending like a mustache from the base of its bill. Their bodies are predominately black but show a great amount of white on the underwings when in flight, especially from the front. The call is a loud resounding *wucka wucka wucka*, similar to the Common Flicker, only it is more emphatic and irregular.

Another identifying characteristic of the Pileated Woodpecker is the rectangular shape and depth (some are several inches deep) of the cavities it excavates in search of wood-boring beetles and carpenter ants. Courtship begins in late winter when the male calls to the female, raises its crest, and bobs its head back and forth. He may open his wings and circle the tree while bobbing. Upon pairing, a joint flight may occur with the male circling the female. Usually four or five white eggs are laid in a nest cavity with incubation taking two to three weeks. The young are fed regurgitated food and leave the nest in about four weeks. However, they may remain with the parents for awhile with both taking care of them.

Although the normal diet of the Pileated Woodpecker is carpenter ants and beetles it readily takes nuts and berries in season. Not only does it tap into standing trees, but it takes apart stumps and logs looking for insects. Occasionally they will take insects from the ground. They can be easily attracted to birdfeeding stations with suet.

Pileated Woodpecker

YELLOW-BELLIED SAPSUCKER

Sphyrapicus varius

The Yellow-bellied Sapsucker is a winter resident in Texas and Oklahoma, migrating from the north. The breeding range of this woodpecker is declining and seems to be limited to the northern tier of eastern states and eastern Canada. Even in some of its original range it is absent. In the southwest, they can be found nearly everywhere there are a few trees. They arrive in Texas and Oklahoma in late September and early October and remain until the following April; some remain into the beginning of May. Two sapsuckers which are similar are the Red-naped Sapsucker and the Red-breasted Sapsucker, both of which have more red and can be found further west. The Red-breasted Sapsucker has an entirely red head and breast. The Red-naped Sapsucker has a red nape which is lacking in the Yellow-bellied Sapsucker.

At only eight inches tall, the Yellow-bellied Sapsucker is not one of the largest of the woodpeckers. Its back is black with white or buff markings. Two white wing patches are prominent both at rest and in flight. Its underside is a pale-yellow, hence the name "yellow-bellied," with some black streaking along its flanks. Both sexes have a black "bib" on the upper chest; the male has a red throat while the female's is white. The facial patterns are similar except for the throat patch. Its forecrown is red-and-black and white stripes mark the rest of its head. From the top of its head to the base of its neck it is black. A small white rump patch is evident in flight but not as strongly as in the Northern Flicker. Their call is a downward slurred *chirrrrr* or sometimes a quick *pee-ek*, which it gives when alarmed in hiding.

The Yellow-bellied Sapsucker makes ring-shaped holes in the cambium of tree. These holes are evenly spaced and the concentric rows of holes are also evenly spaced. This boring is similar to tapping for maple sap to make maple sugar and syrup, hence the name "sapsucker." The Yellow-bellied Sapsucker drinks the sap which flows from the holes but, more importantly, it uses it to lure insects which are then captured and eaten. This bird may make rings of holes on as many as six trees at a time, which it then visits throughout the day to gather the sweet sap and insects. The Yellow-bellied Sapsucker remembers which trees provide the best sap to attract insects and returns year after year to the same tree, although it makes new holes every year. The holes in trees can be seen for scores of years and do not normally damage the tree.

162

Yellow-bellied Sapsucker

EASTERN KINGBIRD   *Tyrannus tyrannus*

In the southwest, the Eastern King-bird is a migratory bird as well as a summer resident. During the winter, it migrates to South America. Except for in Arizona and California, this bird is quite common and during the nesting season can be found in shrubby areas, open fields, open woodlands, and park spaces. Not particularly fond of suburbia, they are not usually found in backyards except where they adjoin a field or a scrubby natural area.

The Eastern Kingbird stands about eight inches tall. It is a striking bird with a black back and white to light-gray undersides. Its tail is black with a conspicuous white band across the very tip. This white band is quite evident when the bird is in flight or hovering. As in many of the kingbirds, there is a characteristic red spot on the top of its head which is seldom seen unless the red crest is in an agitated state. The bill of the Eastern Kingbird has bristles at the base which are not noticeable unless you are very close.

The Eastern Kingbird sits on wires, fences, or posts and flies out to capture insects, often hovering above the prey. It is very feisty and will attack larger birds including hawks, crows, and jays that may threaten their young or nest. While hovering, the Eastern Kingbird's wings beat very fast almost as if they are quivering. When hovering or flying, the Eastern Kingbird makes a rapid series of nasal notes: *kit kit kit kitter kitter*, picking up speed at the end.

Although migrating birds and summer residents begin arriving in March, nesting does not begin until May. The Eastern Kingbird prefers to nest in shrubs, but it has been known to build nests in tall trees. The nest is built on a horizontal branch about midway between the trunk and edge. Another favorite place to nest is out in the open on a post or snag. Adult birds will attack and scold you if you approach the nest too closely.

The nest is made of weeds and grasses and lined with fine grasses and feathers. The light-colored eggs are marked with brown blotches; four eggs are usually laid. Incubation is the duty of the female, and takes two to three weeks. The young are attended by both parents and fledge in two to three weeks. Since only one brood is produced the young may remain with the parents for an extended period of time. By the end of October, the summer residents and migratory kingbirds leave the southwest.

The diet of this bird is predominately insects although some berries are taken. Meal worms will often entice these beautiful birds to a feeder. Occasionally they will become a nuisance as they take honey bees from beehives. This trait has given the Eastern Kingbird the nick name "Bee Martin."

164

Eastern Kingbird

TROPICAL AND WESTERN KINGBIRD
Tyrannus melancholicus / Tyrannus verticalis

These two nine-inch tall birds are very similar in markings and color. Cassin's Kingbird appears to be identical to the Western Kingbird except that it lacks the white outer tail feathers. The Tropical Kingbird appears identical to Couch's Kingbird, but is found only in extreme southern Arizona, whereas Couch's Kingbird is found only in extreme southeastern Texas. All four of these flycatchers have gray heads and black bills with whiskers at the base. Their underbellies are yellow and their backs are olive-gray.

The Western Kingbird can be distinguished by its white outer tail feathers on its black tail. It can be found widely over the entire southwest with the exception of the extreme eastern portions of Texas and Oklahoma. The Tropical Kingbird has no white outer tail feathers and its bill is quite massive in comparison to the Western Kingbird. It also has a slightly-notched tail and its cheek is a bit grayer than that of the Western Kingbird. All the kingbirds mentioned above are summer residents with the exception of Couch's Kingbird which winters in Texas.

Kingbirds are primarily insect-eaters and feed from a perch such as a fence wire or post. Where these are absent, they feed from shrubs and branches extending from trees. When they see an insect they swoop down and take it. In times of abundance they will also take berries and seeds.

The Western Kingbirds prefer a open habitat with scattered shrubs. In the southwest, they prefer semi-open lands, pastures, fields, and wide roadways. In the west, unlike the Eastern Kingbird, they have adapted to living in parks and suburban areas. The Tropical Kingbird, on the other hand, prefers river bottoms where there are many trees, especially cottonwoods. Further south into Mexico and South America, it prefers habitats more like the Western Kingbird.

The Tropical Kingbird builds a nest of twigs, grasses, plant fibers, and bark on horizontal branches. The four or five creamy blotched eggs are incubated for about two weeks by the female. When hatched, the young are attended by both parents who feed for about three weeks before they fledge.

The Western Kingbird nests on horizontal branches but has become quite adapted to manmade structures including poles, ledges, bridges, towers, porches, and other flat areas. Its nest is a large cup made up of a variety of plant materials. The five whitish heavily-blotched eggs are incubated primarily by the female for two to three weeks. The young take another two to three weeks to fledge.

Populations of the Western Kingbird are increasing and individuals have moved eastward as far as Florida to winter. The Tropical Kingbird has been increasing in Arizona and some have even shown up in Texas.

Top: Tropical Kingbird
Bottom: Western Kingbird

GREAT CRESTED FLYCATCHER

Myiarchus crinitus

The Great Crested Flycatcher is about the same general size and shape as the western kingbirds with the exception that its tail is a bit longer giving it a slightly larger look than the kingbirds. The habitat of the Great Crested Flycatcher is woodlands, which in Oklahoma and eastern Texas limits the areas in which it can be found. It is quite common as a nesting bird and is a winter resident in the extreme southern parts of Texas.

This nine-inch bird is black on its head, back, and throat. Its chest and belly are lemon-yellow to the base of its tail. As in the other flycatchers, its bill is fairly large and typically flattened with bristles at the base. The lower mandible may have some yellow in it. Its tail and some of the primary feathers in the wing show a pale-rust in them when in flight. When disturbed or defending its territory, the Great Crested Flycatcher will raise the feathers on its head giving it a distinct crest. The call is a loud guttural *creeep* or *weee* or can be repeated several times: *creep creep creep*. There are two variations of the call: one guttural and the other more melodic and sweet. The melodic sweet call is common in southwestern woodlands during the summer.

A forest bird, the Great Crested Flycatcher nests in tree cavities. It does not excavate the cavity itself but takes over a woodpecker house or uses a naturally-rotted cavity. Its nest is built to within a few inches of the top of the cavity. Nest material almost always includes bits of snakeskin. Not terribly fussy about nesting material it will use whatever is available: fur, feathers, leaves, string, rope, leaves, and other vegetation, as well as pieces of plastic wrap as a snakeskin substitute. Five cream-colored eggs marked with brown are laid in April and are incubated by the female for about two weeks. Both parents will take care of the young after hatching and they fledge in about three weeks. One brood per year is produced.

The Great Crested Flycatcher primarily eats insects from the woodland. It has also been known to eat small lizards, salamanders, and some berries in the fall and during migration. Nest boxes have had some success in attracting the Great Crested Flycatcher when placed in the proper habitat. Occasionally, when a Purple Martin house is overtaken by trees they will attempt to nest in it.

Great Crested Flycatcher

BLACK PHOEBE AND SAY'S PHOEBE

Sayornis nigricans / Sayornis saya

Both of these striking little birds can be found over much of the southwest except for the eastern half of Texas and Oklahoma. The Black Phoebe is limited to California, southern Nevada, Arizona, New Mexico, and Texas.

The Black Phoebe, as its name suggests, is black with a white belly. It is smaller than Say's Phoebe at under seven inches tall. Its call is a four-noted *pee weee*, rising on the first part then descending. It can be found in woodlands near water—in fact it can almost always be found *above* water. It has adapted well to city parks and irrigation waterways made by man. The Black Phoebe sits on a perch and flies out to catch insects. It also may take insects as they emerge from water. Like hawks and owls, these birds cough up pellets of undigested insects.

Its nest is made of mud and placed on the shelf of a cliff or the flat portions of manmade structures, especially bridges. Its nest is lined with grasses and soft plant materials. Four or five whitish eggs are incubated by the female for two to three weeks. The young are attended by both parents for another three weeks before they are able to leave. Two broods, and occasionally three, are reared each year.

Adaptation to human water areas have allowed this bird to increase in some areas and overall their populations are stable. It is a permanent resident in most of the areas in which it nests in the southwest.

Say's Phoebe is a little larger at seven to eight inches tall and is gray-brown overall. Its most identifiable feature is the peach-brown color on the lower front of its body and undertail. Its tail is dark as is its head. The female Vermilion Flycatcher is similar to Say's Phoebe but is lightly streaked below.

Its call is a downward *pee-ee* or *peet-see-ah*. Its preferred habitat is arid or semi-arid open scrub lands, canyons, farms, and ranches. The habitat of Say's Phoebe is completely opposite to that of the Black Phoebe, which prefers areas with water. Its diet is primarily insects taken from a perch. It also coughs up undigested insect parts.

Say's Phoebe places its nest on the horizontal surface of cliffs, caves, branches, or manmade structures. Its nest is relatively flat and is constructed of grasses and plant material. The four white eggs are incubated by the female for two weeks and both parents take care of the young until they are ready to leave the nest in two more weeks. Two broods are common and occasionally a third is possible. This bird has adapted well to suburban landscaping and is increasing over its range. In the southern part of the southwest, it is a permanent resident and migratory over the north.

Top: Black Phoebe
Bottom: Say's Phoebe

VERMILION AND SCISSOR-TAILED
FLYCATCHER *Pyrocephalus rubinus / Tyrannus forficatus*

This six-inch bird is found mostly in Arizona, New Mexico, and Texas although some, especially in migration, are found in California. In Arizona, New Mexico, and Texas it is a permanent resident. The male's head and front to his belly is a bright vermilion-red. His cheek and back is dark-brown, almost black. The female is lighter-brown above and light-gray below with light streaking. The belly of the female has a blush of apricot or peach. The cheek patch in the female is quite pronounced. The song of the male is a dainty *peet a see, peet a see.*

The Vermilion Flycatcher prefers to nest near water including golf courses. It feeds by swooping down from perches to catch insects and coughs up pellets of undigested insects.

The female builds a nest on a horizontal branch between five to twenty feet above the ground. It is small compact cup made from twigs, grass, leaves, and weeds. The inside of the nest is lined with soft plant fibers, hair, and sometimes feathers. Lichens decorate the exterior much like in a hummingbird's nest. Three white eggs with brown spots are incubated, mainly by the female. The eggs hatch in about two weeks and both parents care for the young until they fledge about two weeks later. Two broods per year are common.

The Scissor-tailed Flycatcher is truly unforgettable. This bird is twelve to fifteen inches in length and a soft-gray over its head, upper chest, and back. Its head has the typical red spot. Its wings are black, and its flanks, underwings, and undertail are a dark-peach color and extremely beautiful, especially in flight. It has been said that "You haven't seen a Scissor-tailed Flycatcher until you have seen the pink of the armpits."

This bird is found in Texas, Oklahoma, and parts of Colorado, New Mexico, and Arkansas. It prefers semi-open ranges, ranches, and farmlands. It forages along roadsides where it sits on a fence post or wire and swoops down on insects.

Nesting begins early, with the male doing a magnificent courtship flight. He flies up into the air and descends with his long tail streaming behind him. The male gives sharp calls and may even tumble in some flights. The female builds the nest on a horizontal branch or manmade structure. Its nest is a flat cup of weeds, grass roots, and twigs, and is lined with softer materials. The female will incubate the five brown-spotted eggs for just over two weeks. Both parents will attend the young for about sixteen days until they fledge.

Populations are stable but local populations may vary. Fall brings an influx of migrants in the southwest. The immature birds will occasionally wander and show up most anywhere in the United States. These birds over-winter in Florida and occasionally other areas along the Gulf coast.

Left: Scissor-tailed Flycatcher   Right: Vermilion Flycatcher
                                         Left: Male Right: Female

BARN SWALLOW *Hirundo rustica*

The Barn Swallow is probably the most recognized of all the swallows. This bird has the long divided 'swallow tail' as well as the streamlined body, pointed wings, and swooping graceful flight. These birds are dark-blue above with buff or deep-rust undersides. Young birds are not as rust-colored underneath as the adults. Its throat is a deep mahogany color with a partially blue neck band extending from the back. Its forehead has the same rust color on it as on its breast. In flight, the deeply-forked tail exhibits white spots which make this bird totally different from other swallows.

At about seven inches, the Barn Swallow is not as large as the Purple Martin but it is larger than the Northern Rough-winged Swallow. In flight, the Barn Swallow gives off a series of *szweet szweet* sounds.

The courtship of Barn Swallows is interesting. The pair flies in long drawn-out flights, landing on a wire to continue the courtship. Sitting next to each other they rub, twist their heads together, and preen each other. During courtship, the pair makes a series of twitters and guttural chortles, interspersed with little pops like cracking gum.

In the southwest, the Barn Swallow is found nearly everywhere with the exception of the extremely arid parts of Arizona and California. Since its nest is predominately mud, the lack of these birds in arid areas seems reasonable. Populations seem to be increasing where buildings are available and a friendly host will allow them to stay. Winter is devoid of these birds as they migrate early to Central and South America.

The Barn Swallow typically builds its nest on the beams of barns, ledges or shelves under bridges, in culverts or caves, and on cliffs or in outdoor pavilions. Its nest is constructed of mud pellets cemented together to form a half-cup. It usually takes the parents more than a week to build the nest. The nest is lined with coarse grass and feathers. Old nests are repaired and used again.

Four to five white eggs with brown markings are laid and incubated for about two weeks. The incubation is shared by both sexes. The young are fed regurgitated insects and are able to leave the nest in about three weeks. The last week or so the young have outgrown the nest and will sit around the top of it, from which they often fall or are easily taken by predators. Young birds return to the nest to roost for a short time after fledging. Parent birds will re-nest shortly, often in the same nest. The same families will return to the same successful nesting areas for years.

174

Barn Swallow

WESTERN SCRUB JAY AND STELLAR'S JAY

Aphelocoma californica / Cyanocitta stelleri

Many people find jays a nuisance because they eat everything and are raucous and intimidating to small birds at birdfeeding stations.

The Scrub Jay can be found over most of the southwest except for parts of Arizona, eastern Texas, and Oklahoma. This eleven-inch bird has a blue head and tail. It does not have a crest. Its underbody is light-gray with a necklace of streaks on its throat. Its back is gray. This bird prefers the scrubby foothills of the southwest; it can be found in any brushy open forest habitat and it is becoming prevalent in natural parks. In the southwest, it is a permanent resident although it shifts altitudes and habitats with seasons and food availability.

The diet of the Scrub Jay is pretty much anything it can swallow. During the summer it feeds on insects, other small birds, eggs, rodents, and reptiles. As winter approaches, its diet shifts to seeds, nuts, and berries. The Scrub Jay often hoards food in times of abundance, primarily acorns.

The Scrub Jay's nest is usually found between six to fifteen feet from the ground. Both sexes build a substantial nest of twigs, grass, and moss and line it with finer plant material. Five or six olive-spotted eggs are incubated for just over two weeks by the female while the male feeds her. Both sexes tend the young for another two to three weeks until they are ready to fledge. Occasionally a second brood is raised.

Stellar's Jay is a large bird at thirteen inches. It has a taller crest than the Blue Jay and is dark-blue over most of its body with a black head, neck, and upper breast. Its wings and tail have black bars. In the darker areas of the forest it may even appear totally black. It is found over the entire southwest except in Texas and Oklahoma. Its range stretches northward well into Canada. Its preferred habitat is almost unbroken forests of pines but it also frequents mixed conifer areas and has adapted to city parks and older suburbs where trees have matured. They also frequent birdfeeders, especially after nesting. The call is not the typical raucous *jay* call but an untypical *haack, haack, haack.* Stellar's Jay feeds on seeds, nuts, and berries, as well as insects and small animals.

Its nest is placed relatively high in a tree and is built by both sexes from a grasses, weeds, leaves, and other plant material and lined with softer material. It is cemented together with mud. Four or five blue-green brown-spotted eggs are incubated mainly by the female for two to three weeks. Both parents attend the young for three weeks until they fledge.

Populations are stable and permanent but, similar to the Scrub Jay, they may move during the fall and winter in response to food availability. During the non-breeding season they make up loose flocks, moving and foraging through the dense forests.

Top: Stellar's Jay
Bottom: Scrub Jay

CAROLINA CHICKADEE   *Parus carolinensis*

The Carolina Chickadee is the southern counterpart to the Black-capped Chickadee and they are almost identical with a few minor differences. The most obvious is the call of the Carolina Chickadee which is a loud four-note *fee-bee fee-bay*. The Black-capped Chickadee's call has only two notes: *fee-bee*. The smaller Carolina Chickadee's call, the *dee dee dee dee,* is faster and a bit higher in pitch.

Another minor difference is the line at the bottom of its black bib. The Carolina Chickadee has a rather smooth line, whereas the Black-capped Chickadee has a jagged line. Also, the Carolina Chickadee has no white in its wing which is present in the Black-capped Chickadee. Both birds have a black cap and black bib with a white cheeks. Their backs are brownish-gray and their undersides are light-gray. The Carolina Chickadee is less than five inches long.

The Carolina Chickadee is quite common in Texas, Oklahoma, and Arkansas. It prefers deciduous woodlands, open woodlands, and park lands but will frequent swamps and thickets if nest sites are available. Older suburban neighborhoods are attractive to this little bird as the trees become more mature and people provide birdfeeding stations.

The Carolina Chickadee and the Black-capped Chickadee mate for life and move about in socially structured flocks. Only two or three pairs of the flock are allowed to build a nest and produce young. The nest is in a tree cavity and is excavated by both sexes. It is usually an older cavity started by a woodpecker and enlarged by the chickadees. It is lined with plant down and hair unless the wood pulp is soft enough in itself. Five to seven white eggs are laid and incubated primarily by the female for about two weeks. A loud hiss is given by the brooding birds if they are approached too closely. The young fledge in a little over two weeks. The young stay nearby for a short time and are fed by the parents. With increased nesting areas and nest boxes the populations are stable or increasing slightly.

Carolina Chickadee

TUFTED TITMOUSE *Parus bicolor*

In the southwest, the Tufted Titmouse is found in Texas, Oklahoma, and eastward. In Texas, the Tufted Titmouse has a black crest and is called the Black-crested Titmouse. In Arizona and New Mexico, the Plain Titmouse is found. The Titmouse prefers wood lots and forests, but it can be found in scrub lands and open woodlands. State parks and refuges are good places to find the Tufted Titmouse as well as many backyard birdfeeding stations.

The Tufted Titmouse is a relative of the Chickadees and sports a "tuft," or crest, as its name indicates. At only six inches tall, this little bird looks like a house mouse with its overall gray color and bright black eyes. Its underside is light-colored with rust or brown on the flanks. Its feet and legs are gray; its bill short and black.

This bird gives a clear, loud whistle: *peter peter peter* or *weeder weeder weeder*. Variations are a sweet, loud *trick* or *treat*. When moving through the forest together they will give a little *tseet* similar to that of the Chickadee. If disturbed they will give a scolding, raspy *wheea wheea wheea*.

The Tufted Titmouse is easy to attract to birdfeeding stations. It prefers the gray-striped sunflower, but any sunflower will be taken. Since the Tufted Titmouse doesn't have the capacity to crack open the sunflower, as do the Cardinal and Grosbeak, they take the seed away to a perch and split it open by placing it between their toes and striking it with their beak. Many people put out sunflower chips and hearts so they don't have to work so hard and to lessen the mess left by hulls. During the winter, the Tufted Titmouse will also eat suet, especially a mixture of suet and peanut butter. The Tufted Titmouse can even be taught to eat from your hand.

For its nest the Tufted Titmouse uses a natural cavity or a cavity from a woodpecker. It also uses manmade nest boxes. Nests have been found as low as a couple of feet above the ground to as high as one hundred feet. The nest cavity is lined with moss, bark, leaves, fur, and hair. Fur and hair seem to be so important to the Titmouse that it has been seen taking it from living creatures! Like the Great Crested Flycatcher, it almost always puts snake skins in its nest. Successful nest sites are used year after year.

Five to seven white eggs with small brown markings are incubated by the female for two weeks. Young are attended by both parents for two to three weeks prior to fledging. In the southwest, two broods are sometimes produced; the first attends the young of the second. This bird mates for life and during the winter they can be found in mixed flocks of Chickadees, Nuthatches, and Downy Woodpeckers. Occasionally warblers or kinglets will join the group. They set up a winter feeding territory and remain together as a group until the next breeding season.

Tufted Titmouse

CAROLINA WREN   *Thryothorus ludovicianus*

The Carolina Wren is a woodland bird that breeds throughout Texas and Oklahoma. The Carolina Wren prefers mature open woodlands with abundant understory plants but it has learned to adapt to suburbia, especially near older homes that have well-established trees and shrubs. It will nest in wood lots adjoining agricultural areas.

This wren is five to six inches in length and is a dark reddish-brown above and a buff-cream on its chest and belly. Its wing bars are a faint row of white dots. Its tail is usually held erect and has faint bars across the feathers. Its head has a pronounced white eye-stripe bordered by black stripes above and below it. Its bill is long, pointed, and slightly downcurved. Its throat is white.

For such a small bird it is quite loud, possibly so that it can be heard in the deep forest. The most common call is a loud *teakettle teakettle teakettle* repeated over and over again. Occasionally, a two-note call will be given: *churry churry churry*. When disturbed or scolding, the Carolina Wren gives a *pishhhing* call. When other birds hear it they come to investigate and chime in. Birders imitate this call, causing birds to show themselves and as more birds come and scold, a snowballing effect occurs, attracting even more birds. The *pishhhing* call or playing bird tapes are not to be overused or used in the breeding season because they stress the birds. Many parks, refuges, and natural areas have outlawed the use of tapes and before using them you should check the regulations.

The nest of the Carolina Wren is placed in a variety of places. Traditionally they prefer cavities but they will use any nook or cranny to place a nest. One of their favorites in a suburban yard is a hanging basket or flower pot. In the wild they will use stumps, woodpecker holes, upturned tree roots, and spaces between rocks. The nest is constructed of twigs, leaves, roots, and bark strips. When possible, the nest is domed so that the entrance is from the side. The lining is finer materials such as grass, hair, moss, fur, and feathers. Both parents construct the nest but the female is attended by the male as she incubates the eggs for about two weeks.

The eggs are cream-colored with brown markings. Both parents attend the young until fledging two weeks later. Often young birds will remain with the male as the female begins to build another nest. In the southwest, two broods are common and a third brood is possible on occasion.

Carolina Wren

CANYON WREN *Catherpes mexicanus*

The Canyon Wren is also almost six inches in length and is found over the entire southwest except from east Texas eastward. As its name indicates it prefers rock-walled canyons, draws, and steep-walled stream sides. It builds its nest on stone buildings in the correct habitat. During non-nesting times, it can be found in other habitats as well.

The Canyon Wren has a long downcurved bill. Its throat and breast are white and its back, tail, and undersides are a rich-brown with white spotting accented with black. Its tail is barred. Its call, which is the easiest way to identify this bird, is a series of loud clear descending whistles. Its call bounces off canyons walls and can be heard for great distances. If you hear one, look for a rock outcropping on which he will often be sitting out in the open singing his heart out. The rest of the time he is very secretive and mouse-like, hiding in the brush and rock crevices.

The Canyon Wren, like most of the wrens, eats mostly insects and other invertebrates. It takes ants, beetles, leaf-eating insects, and spiders by using its long bill to probe in the crevices of rocks. It hops around and often hangs upside down underneath the rocks while investigating them for food. Although it forages on logs, it rarely feeds from trees or shrubs.

This permanent resident begins nesting in early spring with the male defending a territory with his beautiful call. Both sexes build a nest in a hole between rocks, a stump, or in a deep crevice. The nest is first lined with twigs and then with softer materials such as moss and plant down. Often times the nest is reused several times. Five white eggs are incubated by the female while the male defends the territory and feeds her. The period of incubation is about eighteen days. The young are attended by both parents and grow quickly, being able to leave the nest in about two weeks; longer if it is a larger brood.

In wild canyons and where there is minimal human habitation this pretty little bird is holding its own. Where humans interfere, the populations may be on the decline.

Canyon Wren

CACTUS WREN *Campylorhynchus brunneicapillus*

The Cacus Wren is the largest wren in the United States at well over eight inches tall. This bird is synonymous with the cactus country of the southwest. It is a common permanent resident of the desert regions of Texas, New Mexico, Arizona, California, and parts of Nevada and Utah. Brown overall, this bird is heavily streaked over most of its body with a lighter buff beneath. Its crown is black or dark brown and heavy white pronounced eye-stripe is prominent. Its throat is heavily streaked, making it appear from a distance as if its throat is completely dark. Its bill is deeply curved and black. Its tail is relatively long and barred.

The preferred habitat of the Cactus Wren is the desert, but it may be found in mixed desert locations and other arid areas. It has adapted well to communities that have overtaken the desert, even frequenting birdfeeders. Populations are stable and most abundant in deserts with cactus, especially the cholla cactus. This bird is best known for its loud raspy calls, a rapid drawn out *cha cha cha cha cha cha.* The calls can be heard anytime of the day or year. Often it is the first bird we wake up to in the morning, along with Gambel's Quail.

Living in the desert, the Cactus Wren feeds mainly on insects but during seasonal abundance it takes seeds and cactus fruit. It takes nectar from cactus flowers as well as insects hiding in the flowers and feeds on the ground as well. In addition, Cactus Wrens have been observed feeding on smashed bugs on car grills, going so far as creeping behind the grill guard to pick insects from the radiator!

Cactus Wrens mate for life and remain in a territory for several years. The male builds a number of dummy nests which is characteristic of many wrens and the female will select the one she wishes to use. The nest is a huge ball of plant materials usually placed in a cholla cactus or dense shrub. The nest is horizontally-shaped and the entrance gives on to a passageway that leads to the center. The inside is lined with plant down, feathers and hair. The nests are not hidden at all, possibly because the cholla cactus makes a formidable fortress.

The female incubates the four brown-spotted whitish eggs for sixteen days. Three weeks later the young are able to leave the nest, but will remain in the area for a time.

Cactus Wren

NORTHERN MOCKINGBIRD   *Mimus polyglottos*

The Northern Mockingbird is the bird most often recognized by southwestern residents as being a common permanent resident. This bird belongs to the group of birds called the "mimic thrushes" because they reproduce the sounds of other birds and a variety of other creatures quite accurately. The mimic calls can be so accurate it is almost impossible to differentiate them from the real thing. The Mockingbird usually gives the call in groups of three or more, the Catbird does not repeat them but keeps adding new calls, and the Brown Thrasher makes the call twice.

The Northern Mockingbird is ten inches long and slender with a long tail. It is predominately gray on the upper parts of its body with white underneath. Its tail is bordered by white feathers and there are large splashes of white in its wings while in flight. Its wings have two wing bars and some of the white spots are visible when they are folded.

The Mockingbird is a common resident of suburbia as well as most parks or wayside areas. The Mockingbird has adapted well to agricultural areas and can be found in most edge or transitional habitats. It prefers to nest in shrubs about five to eight feet above the ground, rarely exceeding ten feet. The nest is rather bulky with a base of twigs, built mainly by the male and lined with rootlets, fine leaves, grass, and other soft plant material by the female.

The three to five light-greenish-blue eggs are speckled with blotches of brown. The eggs are incubated for twelve to thirteen days before hatching. Two weeks later the young will fledge. Both parents attend the young.

During courtship, the male and female do a mating dance on the ground with their heads and tails erect and wings spread. They run toward each other and then retreat. Then they repeat the run, sometimes flying into the air. Unsuccessful males will continue to sing to attract a female into the late hours of the night. In the southwest, nesting begins in March and continues into late summer with up to four broods.

The Northern Mockingbird is fond of almost any fruit or insect. Mockingbirds have a unique way of capturing insects called "hawking." They give a "wing flash"—a sudden, quick rising of the wings to flash the white in them as they walk on the ground. Then they slowly lower their wings to watch for any insect startled by this movement.

The Northern Mockingbird can be enticed to feeders with fruit, cooked vegetables, suet, or insects. During the winter, the population of the Mockingbird swells with northern migrants.

Northern Mockingbird

CRISSAL THRASHER *Toxostoma crissale*

The Crissal Thrasher is one of the largest and most striking of the thrashers. At twelve or more inches in length, this bird is found in the desert regions of Texas, New Mexico, Arizona, and California. It can also be found in a few local places in Nevada and Utah. The bill of this thrasher is notably shorter than some others but is heavily curved downward. Its upper body is dark-brown and its lower body is a soft warm-brown. Its face has a dark whisker streak with faint streakings on its cheeks. Its undertail coverts are rich-mahogany, striking and characteristic if you can see it, and similar to the Gray Catbird's undertail coverts. The call of the Crissal Thrasher is a slow repeated *chicadeery* or *pecaaary*. Of course, being a thrasher, it mimics the calls of other birds as well.

The Crissal Thrasher is very secretive, hiding in dense shrubs and thickets. It often sits high up in shrubs or trees and sings.This bird can be located by listening during the morning and evening hours. It can be found in brushy mountainside areas, near streams, or other water.

Insects make up the greatest portion of the Crissal Thrasher's diet. It hops along the ground and uses its curved pointed bill to probe the earth, turning over leaves, small branches, and dung to locate insects. In season it takes fruits and berries. Sometimes it takes small lizards and bird's eggs.

Pairs mate, possibly for life; at the very least they will defend a territory for a year. Its nest is well-hidden in low shrubs, usually two to four feet above the ground. The nest is bulky, with heavy twigs making up the infrastructure and lined with softer grasses, leaves, and grass. Three unmarked blue-green eggs are incubated by both parents for two weeks. Although the young are able to leave the nest after two more weeks, they will remain and be fed by the adults until they can fly with some assurance. Two broods each year are common.

Populations of the Crissal Thrasher are stable but not terribly abundant for this permanent resident.

Crissal Thrasher

CURVE-BILLED THRASHER *Toxostoma curvirostre*

In the southwest, the Curve-billed Thrasher is probably the most often seen and recognized bird. It is not as timid as some of the other thrashers and often sits high in a cactus or shrub singing incessantly. It has also adapted well to suburbia, living in backyards in arid country. At just over eleven inches, the Curve-billed Thrasher is a mottled buff-gray on the breast and soft-gray on the back. Its wings have two faint wing bars and a darker tail. The eye is a light-orange and the bill is curved downward. The tail spots are usually inconspicuous.

The call of the Curve-billed Thrasher is a loud sharp *whit whit* or *whit whee*. The mating call is a variety of harmonious calls, given in series, often copying a variety of bird and insect sounds.

The Curve-billed Thrasher is common in the right habitats of Arizona, New Mexico, Texas, and parts of southern Colorado. It is found in mixed areas of cactus and mesquite as well as chaparral, or where there is a large variety of vegetation that does not extend too far up the mountain sides.

Insects make up the greatest portion of the Curve-billed Thrasher's diet. It uses its long downcurved bill as a pry bar to turn over leaves, sticks, and other debris to find beetles, grasshoppers, ants, and leaf insects. During extremely dry periods, when the ground is hard it will use its bill as a chisel. An opportunist, it will also take snails and spiders. During the season, it feeds heavily on berries and the fruit of the prickly pear and saguaro cacti. In many areas, it has adapted to birdfeeders and watering stations. It is especially attracted to moving water and misters.

The Curved-billed Thrasher seems to mate and defend a territory for an entire year. Its favorite nesting spot is the cholla cactus, where it sometimes finds itself in heavy competition with the Cactus Wren. In fact, the Thrasher will destroy any encroaching Cactus Wren's nest. The Thrasher is not too proud to raid the nests of other birds in the area. The nest is built by both birds, occasionally using an old nest of a dove or Cactus Wren. The base of the nest is thorny twigs and is lined with grasses, feathers, hair, and soft down. The pale green eggs are spotted with brown and the incubation begins with the first egg laid. Incubation lasts for two weeks and the eggs hatch over a period of days. As the young reach two to three weeks old they fledge. Two broods are common, with an occasional third.

Texas populations may be on the decline but in Arizona the Curve-billed Thrasher is doing quite well.

Curve-billed Thrasher

AMERICAN ROBIN *Turdus migratorius*

Called the "Robin Redbreast" by school children, this bird is one of the most numerous winter visitors in the southwest. In the last fifty years, it has become a fairly substantial breeder in suburban areas in Arizona, California, and Texas. The American Robin can be found wherever there are berries.

At ten inches tall, the American Robin is the largest thrush. The back of the American Robin is brownish-black and its head and tail are gray-black. Its throat is white with fine black streaking. Its eye has a broken white ring around it. Its chest and part of its belly are brick-red with a white lower belly. Its bill is yellow. In flight, its tail flashes white at the outer tips.

The American Robin typically hops about the lawn with its head cocked to one side looking for worms, a favorite spring and summer food. Many people think when they see the Robin's head cocked to one side, it is listening intently for worms. Actually it is looking down a worm hole for a bit of shiny worm to strike and grab.

Female American Robins are not as brightly colored, but sometimes during nesting it may be difficult to tell them apart. The Robin's call is a familiar spring song and it has a number of phrases such as *cheer up, cheerie lee, cheerie ly*—all given in succession with a definite pause between them. The Robins are the first to sing in the morning and the last to sing at night. A pre-dawn chorus of Robins is a sure sign of spring. When disturbed or angry, the American Robin will give a *tut tut tut* or a loud *peak peak peak.*

March is the earliest that the American Robin nests in the southwest. The nesting continues until early summer, producing two to three broods. Nests are made of twigs, grasses, weeds, string, and bark. The nest is lined with mud to conform to the body of the female and then lined with finer grasses.The nests are placed on a substantial limb or at the joint of a limb, on the ledges of buildings with some protection, and on porch columns and porch lights. Many people provide robin shelves for them to nest upon, which are also good for Eastern Phoebes and Barn Swallows.

Four or five blue eggs are incubated for about two weeks by the female. The young grow quickly on a diet of high-protein insects and can leave the nest in about sixteen days. The young follow the parents around for a few days.

In certain parts of the country, the American Robin is a pest in fruit orchards and vegetable crops. The Robin was one of the indicating birds illustrating the dramatic effects of using unrestricted widespread pesticides.

American Robin

BLUE-GRAY GNATCATCHER *Polioptila caerulea*

The southwest is the wintering ground for a fair number of Blue-gray Gnatcatchers that nest in the north but there is also a growing resident population throughout California, Arizona, and Texas. The Blue-gray Gnatcatcher is found as far north as Maine and west to California. It winters in the southern coastal states and Florida down to Central and South America.

At four to five inches long, this little bird appears to be mostly tail. The male is blue-gray above with light-gray underparts. Its tail is long and has white outer tail feathers. The female is a lighter gray on her back and lacks the dark eye-stripe of the male. Both sexes have white eye-rings. These birds are most often seen flitting about capturing food or collecting nest material. Their long tail seems to be in constant movement.

The Blue-gray Gnatcatcher's call is a somewhat buzzy-sounding *zzee* which is repeated often and constantly. It also calls when returning to its nest so it is fairly simple to locate it. The nest of the Blue-gray Gnatcatcher is extremely intricate. It is quite small, usually little more than an inch across. It is normally placed on a horizontal branch or in the fork of a branch between five to twenty-five feet above the ground. It resembles a hummingbird's nest in that it is compact and made from plant down and spider silk. The outside is covered with lichens to camouflage it

so that it resembles just another knot on the branch. The inside is lined with fine plant material and more down.

The female lays four or five pale-blue eggs with small brown markings. Both parents incubate the eggs which hatch in about twelve days. In two weeks, the young leave and in the southwest a second brood may be produced. With the fragmentation of forests, the Blue-gray Gnatcatcher has become increasingly threatened by Cowbird predation.

The habitat of the Blue-gray Gnatcatcher is quite varied but they prefer woodlands near water. City and state parks are good spots to sight these little birds. Their diet is predominately insects and other small invertebrates. Their bill is quite long and pointed and is adapted to taking small insects.

In California, Arizona, New Mexico, and Texas, the Black-tailed Gnatcatcher can also be found. It is similar in size and description to the Blue-gray Gnatcatcher except its tail is black and the bird is darker overall. Most of this bird's range extends into Mexico where it prefers desert-type habitats.

Blue-gray Gnatcatcher

CEDAR WAXWING   *Bombycilla cedrorum*

The Cedar Waxwing does not nest in the southwest but can be found here most of the year. It is most abundant during the winter migration from October until late April. Cedar Waxwings spend the winter in huge flocks wherever berries and insects can be found. When the food is gone they leave. A favorite place to see these beautiful birds is along ponds, rivers, and other waterways where they sit on a branch along the shore, flitting out to capture insects arising from or descending to the water.

The Cedar Waxwing, at seven inches in length, is exquisite. Its body is a rich light-brown with its underbelly grading to a pale-yellow. Its wings are gray-brown and some secondary feathers on the wings are tipped with a waxy-red color, hence the name "Waxwing." Its tail has a bright-yellow band across the end. Its head is crested with a black facial mask partially bordered by white stripes.

The call of the Cedar Waxwing is a high pitched twitter or *zeee* given in flight and when foraging. When a flock takes off in flight they all begin calling as if saying "OK, guys! Lets go!" The Cedar Waxwing is a very communal bird. During the non-breeding season, it creates huge feeding flocks which can number into the hundreds. In these flocks the Cedar Waxwing is quite tame and can be approached very closely. Even during the nesting season they remain in small colonies, sometimes nesting in the same tree or group of trees. When feeding in these nesting groups, they will leave together and return together. When fledged, the young become part of this group, which may then combine with a couple of other smaller nesting colonies.

The diet of the Cedar Waxwing is primarily berries and insects. The bill of the Cedar Waxwing is relatively small but its gape is fairly large. Initially the young are fed insects, but berries are added to their diet as they become older. After the ice thaws, the crab apples and cranberries ferment and the Cedar Waxwing, after devouring them, can become quite a lush. It is not uncommon to see them lying about the tree in various stages of inebriation!

The mating dance, or "side hop," is elaborate. One bird picks up a berry and sidles up to the prospective mate. It then hops a couple of hops away, then hops back again, passing the berry to the other bird. The prospective mate then hops sideways a couple of hops and then hops back and hands the berry back. This "side hopping" can be repeated for weeks. There is nothing funnier than to see a tree full of Cedar Waxwings, all engaged in doing the "side hop."

Cedar Waxwing

PHAINOPEPLA AND PYRRHULOXIA

Phainopepla nitens / Cardinalis sinuatus

This crested black bird is some times called the "Black Cardinal" although it is not related to the cardinal but rather to the waxwing and flycatchers. At almost eight inches tall, the male Phainopepla is an shiny blue-black bird with a red eye. Its primary feathers show white while in flight. The female's coloration is duller. It is found in New Mexico where it is a permanent resident. In the extreme southwestern tip of Texas it is a summer resident.

Similar to the waxwing, it relies heavily on berries and fruit but it also eats a fair amount of insects. A symbiotic relation exists between the poison ivy plant and the Phainopepla which eats the berries but isn't affected by them. In turn, the seeds are passed through its intestine and redeposited to grow another poison ivy plant. The Phainopepla congregates in small flocks to feed on fruit and berries after the breeding season.

In the southwest, the Phainopepla prefers arid regions of scrub, brush, mesquite, and oak forests. It wanders as the food supply becomes depleted. During the breeding season it takes more insects and ranges shorter distances. It catches insects by dashing out from a perch to catch the bug in midair.

Courtship is also similar to the waxwing with the male feeding the female. He also makes aerial flights displaying for the female. The nest is usually hidden in a bunch of mistletoe, poison ivy, or shrubs. The male builds the nest and shares the incubation of the three gray lavender-spotted eggs with the female. The eggs take about two weeks to hatch and the young leave the nest in three weeks. Two broods are common.

The Pyrrhuloxia, or "Yellow-billed Cardinal," is found in the extreme parts of Arizona, New Mexico, and Texas in scrub, mesquite, and mixed deserts. It has also adapted to suburbs, agricultural areas, and city parks. Its size and shape are similar to the Northern Cardinal but with some major differences. Its bill is bright-yellow and curves downward, giving it a parrot-like appearance. The birds are a soft-gray overall with the male sporting a red crest, face, and breast. Its wings show some red in them. The female lacks most of the red but has some in her crest. Its call is thinner and shorter than that of the Northern Cardinal.

The Pyrrhuloxia eats insects and seeds. It seems to like sunflowers and can be readily attracted to feeders.

Its nest is usually placed in a thicket or shrub. The loose cup is constructed of twigs and heavy weeds and is lined with grasses, bark strips, and fine plant material. The pale-white eggs are spotted with brown and are incubated by the female for two weeks. The young leave the nest in ten to twelve days. Three or four young are the usual for any successful nesting.

Top: Phainopepla
Left: Female Right: Male

Bottom: Pyrrhuloxia
Left: Female Right: Male

201

NORTHERN CARDINAL *Cardinalis cardinalis*

Probably no bird creates more excitement at a backyard birdfeeding station than the Northern Cardinal. It is common throughout Texas, and parts of New Mexico, Arizona, and Nevada. Its preferred habitat is the edges of forested areas, brushy areas, park lands, cemeteries—and increasingly the suburban backyard. Even though the Northern Cardinal is considered a permanent resident, an influx of northern-raised birds move into the southwest for the winter.

The male Cardinal is bright-red overall, including his bill, with a black mask and pronounced crest. The female is predominately buff-brown with red on her wings, crest, breast, tail, and bill. Juveniles lack the red bill and are brown overall. Its bill is massive, sharply-pointed, and resembles a short ice-cream cone.

The song of the Northern Cardinal is a loud and cheerful *what-cheer what-cheer what-cheer, cheer cheer cheer, wheet wheet wheet, purdy purdy purdy*, or any combination of these. In certain locales, very specific dialects are learned. In one small village in the Smoky Mountains male Northern Cardinals supposedly say *whirlpool whirlpool whirlpool*. As permanent residents, the Cardinals are among the first birds to sing during the spring. There are three birds from which you can learn the *chip* notes: the Yellow-rumped Warbler, the Common Yellowthroat, and the Northern Cardinal. The *chip* is sharp and fairly loud. As the Northern Cardinal moves around and feeds, they use this *chip* to keep track of each other. Once you have learned it, you will not forget it.

The courtship rituals of the Northern Cardinals are interesting. Both sexes sing, but the female's song is softer and she accompanies the male. When courtship begins, the male entices her with a seed morsel, which she takes from his mouth. Many would call this kissing. Occasionally these paired birds can be seen singing softly together with crests raised, swaying back and forth as in a duet.

The Cardinal builds its nest in a shrub or small tree. Typically its nest is about four to six feet from the ground, occasionally ten to twelve feet. The nest is well-hidden but loosely built of twigs, weed stems, bark, grasses, leaves, and roots. The inner nest is lined with hair and fine grasses. Three to five bluish-green eggs marked with brown are normal. Incubation is shared by both parents for twelve days. Young are fed a variety of insects, seeds, berries, and fruit. The young leave the nest in about twelve days. Up to four broods are raised in the southwest, less in the north. While the female is on a second nest the male will continue to feed the fledged young.

Northern Cardinal
Top: Male Bottom: Female

LOGGERHEAD SHRIKE *Lanius ludovicianus*

The "Butcher Bird" is another name for the Loggerhead Shrike, a permanent resident of the southwest. During the winter, populations from the north greatly increase their numbers. The habitat of the Loggerhead Shrike is open country with scattered trees and shrubs, scrub lands, open forests, and natural park lands. In areas of concentrated development, the population is declining, possibly due to the loss of habitat and food sources.

The Loggerhead Shrike is a stockier bird than the Northern Mockingbird, with which it is often confused. The Loggerhead Shrike is about nine inches long and primarily gray in color. Its wings and tail are black with the undersides an off-white. Small white wing spots are visible in flight and slightly so while at rest. Its outer tail feathers are also white. The most striking feature of the Loggerhead Shrike is its head. It has a black mask above its bill, unlike the Northern Shrike, and it has a dark hooked bill that it uses to catch prey. When it flies, the white in its wings is not as noticeable as the white in the Mockingbird's wings. Although the Loggerhead Shrike is a ferocious predator, it doesn't have the grasping ability of owls and hawks.

The Loggerhead Shrike feeds on grasshoppers, crickets, mice, small lizards and, if the opportunity arises, small birds and nestlings. One unique feature of shrikes is that they "store" food by impaling it on a thorn bush or barbed wire fence. This cache of food is used when young are being fed or the female is on nest.

The Loggerhead Shrike begins nesting in March. Its nest is placed in a shrub or sometimes a small thick tree. Usually it is placed between five to fifteen feet above the ground. The nest is well constructed of twigs, bark, weed stems, and sticks. The inner lining is grass, plant down, feathers, and rootlets. The male brings the materials but the female does the bulk of the construction.

The female also incubates the eggs as the male brings her tender morsels. Incubation of the five gray eggs marked with black or dark-gray lasts about sixteen days. The male and female both take care of the young until they fledge at three weeks, but it may be several weeks before the young can take care of themselves. Up to three broods can be raised in the southwest.

Loggerhead Shrike

YELLOW WARBLER *Dendroica petechia*

Suburbia has usurped the wetlands and wild areas that used to cover the eastern part of North America. Because of this, some of our wetland birds have had to adjust to life in our shrubby backyards and neighborhoods. The Yellow Warbler is one of these welcome additions to our backyard habitats.

The Yellow Warbler is a yellow bird with a gray-olive back. The male has rust or brown streaks running down its breast. The male sings loudly from trees and shrubs most of the day. His song is three or four notes followed by three quick notes. A common mnemonic is *sweet sweet sweet I'm so sweet*. The song is musical, loud, and easily remembered.

This tame little bird can be found over much of the United States. In the southwest, the Yellow Warbler is primarily a bird of the spring and fall when it migrates through the southwest. It winters from Mexico to South America. In parts of Arizona and California, the Yellow Warbler can be either a permanent resident or winter resident

The nests of the Yellow Warbler are placed in thick shrubs at about eye level. It is very defensive and steadfast in protecting its nest, resisting flight until absolutely necessary which makes it easy to study and admire. If you don't approach too closely it will go about its business of rearing its young and you can see the entire process from incubation to fledging.

Usually four or five off-white eggs with variable brown spots are laid and hatch in about twelve days. The nests are easy to find and are often parasitized by the Brown-headed Cowbird. If the warbler finds the eggs of the Brown-headed Cowbird, it will build another nest over them to prevent them from hatching, giving a "layered look" to the nest. Even so, the Cowbird is still successful enough to cause problems for this little warbler. If hatched, the Cowbird young drive out the other babies and take all the food and energy the parent birds can provide.

An insect eater, the Yellow Warbler gleans insects from vegetation, trees, and shrubs. Occasionally a few berries will be taken.

Yellow Warbler

YELLOW-BREASTED CHAT AND COMMON YELLOWTHROAT *Icteria virens / Geothlypis trichas*

At about eight inches tall, the Chat is the largest of the warblers. It is bright-yellow on its belly and a greenish-brown above. Its belly and undertail coverts are white. Its head is dark with white spectacles and a white whisker line. Its tail is relatively long and rounded at the end. It is common over the southwest in the correct habitat although it is shy and secretive. Its call is a weird collection of garbled caws, hoots, barks, and whistles. It can also make some pretty calls during a mating display flight, when it flutters up into the air.

The Yellow-breasted Chat prefers dense vegetation where it can hide. It eats berries, fruit, and lots of insects. They can be attracted to birdfeeders with a mixture of peanut butter and suet mixed with some grain. In the southwest, water is also a great attractant. In the southwest, it is a summer resident.

Its nest is hidden in dense bushes and is constructed of leaves, grass, and weeds and lined with shredded bark, grasses, and soft plant material. The four cream-colored brown-spotted eggs are incubated by the female for eleven days. The young grow rapidly and are able to leave the nest about nine days later. Two broods are common. In the southwest, populations have declined where its habitat has been decreased.

The Common Yellowthroat is almost a miniature Chat in appearance. In the south it is predominately a sum-

mer resident, but in Texas and other local areas it is a winter resident. It has adapted to shrub lands and semi-prairie areas due to the loss of its wetland habitat.

The Common Yellowthroat is tiny at just five inches but it makes itself known by its color and call. Its back is a dark olive-yellow and its breast a bright-yellow. The male has a black mask which is absent in the female, but she has a faint white eyering. The call is a loud *whitchity whitchity witchity* given by the male throughout the day. In the marsh, the male can be seen sitting atop the cattails with his head tilted back just letting loose with all his might. The call note is a distinctive deep *chuck* which doesn't sound as if it comes from a bird at all.

Its nest is well-hidden at the base of a bunch of dense shrubs, cattails, or other vegetation. The nest is woven with grasses, weed stems, bark strips, and marsh ferns. The inner nest is lined with finer grasses, hair, and fine bark strips. The female constructs the nest and incubates the five creamy-white eggs marked with brown flecks that hatch in twelve days. Both parents feed the fast-growing youngsters a high protein mixture of insects and they fledge in about twelve days. The young will follow the parents for a few days and be fed, the later broods may even migrate with the parents. Two broods are com

Top: Common Yellowthroat
Bottom: Yellow-breasted Chat

PAINTED REDSTART AND BLACK-THROATED GRAY WARBLER

Myioborus pictus / Dendroica nigrescens

The Painted Redstart is a very pretty warbler. It is found only in the mountains of Arizona and New Mexico as a summer resident. Both sexes of the Painted Redstart have the same coloration. Its body is mostly black with a bright-red belly. Its wings have two prominent white patches with its outer tail feathers being white as well. The Painted Redstart flashes its wings and tail to show off, tilting its body and spreading its wings back and forth to display itself, even when foraging. Its diet is predominately insects but it will come to nectar feeders as well as peanut butter.

The Painted Redstart nests on the ground in vegetation along steep canyon walls and cliff overhangs. Its nest is a cup constructed by the female from grass, pine needles, weeds, and bark. The inner lining is hair, fur, and fine grasses. Four creamy-colored spotted eggs are incubated by the female for about two weeks. The young are attended by both parents and two additional weeks are needed before fledging. Two broods are common.

The Black-throated Gray Warbler is found from New Mexico north to Colorado, west to the California coast, and north to British Columbia. In these areas it is a summer breeding bird, but in parts of southern Arizona it can be a permanent resident. The Black-throated Gray Warbler is five inches in length. Its head and neck are black with a white eye-stripe and white whiskers. Its flanks are streaked white and its undersides are primarily white. Its back is streaked with gray. It has a yellow spot between its eye and its bill. Females are a bit more drab. Their song is a buzzy *weedle weedle weedle weet.*

This warbler prefers semi-arid oak forests, mixed woods, and wooded brushlands, particularly oak and pinyon forests. In these areas, it feeds on insects on leaves or from the air.

In the southwest, nesting begins in March with the male setting up a territory. Nest building is done by both birds on a horizontal branch from five to ten feet above the ground. The nest is built of grasses and weeds and lined with finer grasses, fur, hair, and moss. Four or five creamy-white spotted eggs are incubated by the female for about a week. The young are attended by the parents for a couple of weeks before fledging. Normally one brood is produced. The migration of this bird is early for the spring nesting season and late in the fall.

Top: Black-throated Gray Warbler
Bottom: Painted Redstart

211

WESTERN TANAGER AND SUMMER TANAGER *Piranga ludoviciana / Piranga rubra*

The Western Tanager is a bright lime-yellow over most of its body with a brilliant red head. Its wings, tail, and back are black with two prominent yellow wing bars. The female lacks the red head and is not as strikingly yellow or black. Females resemble oriole females but have much more massive and thicker bills. Their song is similar to the robin's except it is thinner and faster. The Western Tanager is found in New Mexico and Arizona northward to upper Canada. It can be found locally in California and the extreme southwestern part of Texas. It prefers open forests, forest edges, riparian forests, and park lands. Usually this bird winters in the tropics but a few remain in California.

Insects make up the greatest portion of its diet but it also eats berries and fruit. It catches insects by gleaning the tops of trees.During the spring, it visits flowers taking nectar, insects, and spiders.

The male arrives first in the spring, quickly followed by the female. He sets up a territory and nest building begins. It prefers conifers and deciduous trees for its nest which is placed on a horizontal branch or fork between twenty to sixty feet above the ground. The nest is made from twigs, grass, and weeds and is lined by the female with finer grasses, rootlets, hair and fur. Five pale blue-green eggs marked with brown are incubated by the female for about two weeks. The nestlings are fed by the parents for an-other two weeks before leaving the nest.

The Summer Tanager is the most common Tanager in the southwest being found in Oklahoma, Texas, New Mexico, Arizona and locally in California. It is red overall and can be mistaken from a distance as a male Cardinal. Females are lime-yellow or green and blend in very well with green foliage. Its call is also robin-like although it is slower than the other tanagers. In the southwest, it prefers both open or dense forests, river bottoms, and lower mountain forests. In the forests, it finds the insects that make up the bulk of the diet. In early spring, it feeds lower in the trees but as the season progresses it forages higher up. Berries are a significant part of its diet during the season. Summer Tanagers have been known to feed at bee hives, taking bees as they leave the hive. Occasionally they will take apart a wasp nest to feed upon the adults and larvae.

A loosely-constructed nest is made from grasses, weeds, bark strips, and mosses and lined with fine grasses. Four to five blue-green spotted eggs are incubated by the female for twelve days. Both sexes are in attendance after hatching. The young leave the nest after a couple of weeks.

Populations have declined in some parts of the southwest but seem to be stable eastward. Some wandering indicates that the northern range may be expanding.

Top: Western Tanager   Bottom: Summer Tanager
Back: Female Front: Male   Back: Female Front: Male

HEPATIC TANAGER *Piranga flava*

The Hepatic Tanager resembles the Summer Tanager with some coloration differences. Both male birds are red overall but the Hepatic Tanager is darker and has a dark ear patch. The bills are also different. The bill of the Summer Tanager is yellow whereas the Hepatic Tanager's bill is dark gray. The female Hepatic Tanager also has a darker ear patch, dark gray bill, and her throat is a brighter yellow. The flanks of the female Hepatic Tanager are light-gray instead of lime-yellow like the Summer Tanager. Both birds are about seven inches in length. Their call is similar to the Grosbeaks but choppier. The call note is a single *chuck* or *check*.

Not as widespread as the two previous Tanagers, the Hepatic Tanager is found only in Arizona, New Mexico, locally in California and in extreme southwestern Texas. The Hepatic Tanager prefers mountain forests of conifers or mixed conifers and oaks. It breeds at elevations higher than the Summer Tanager. It forages high up in the trees where it patiently examines every leaf and twig for worms and other insects. In Mexico and its wintering areas, fruit and berries make up a more significant part of its diet.

Nesting occurs in the mixed forests on a branch of a pine, oak, or sycamore. Its nest is placed beween twenty to fifty feet above the ground on a horizontal branch away from the trunk of the tree. The base structure of the nest is made from weeds and grasses and it is lined with finer grasses and soft plant material. The male brings the building materials but it is the female who builds the nest. The four bluish-green eggs spotted with brown are incubated by the female and it is believed that the eggs hatch in about thirteen days. Both parents attend the young until fledging.

Cowbird parasitism may be one cause for this bird's decline in some southwestern areas. The populations may also fluctuate due to climate.

Hepatic Tanager
Left: Female Right: Male

BLACK-HEADED AND BLUE GROSBEAK

Pheucticus melanocephalus / Guiraca caerulea

The Black-headed Grosbeak is found only in New Mexico, Arizona, and California north into Canada. The male has a black head, its neck and breast is an orange-buff color. Its tail is black with extensive white bars and its wings black with white markings. The female is brown where the male is black with buff striping on her head. Both sexes show yellow wing linings in flight. Its song is similar to the robin's but faster. The call note is a sharp *peek*.

Its preferred habitat is forested areas of river valleys and hillsides where they prefer deciduous trees. Their large bill allows them to crack seeds but insects and berries are the main part of their diet.

Nesting season begins with the male doing aerial displays for the female while singing a melodic song. The nest is built in a deciduous tree about ten to twenty feet above the ground. It is constructed by the female of twigs, weeds, and rootlets and lined with grasses, finer rootlets and hair. The four or five pale-green eggs are marked with beautiful mahogany spots and are incubated jointly for two weeks. The young are not able to fly for another two weeks. During this time they are vulnerable as they wait to be fed. One brood each year is usually produced.

The Blue Grosbeak is small at only six inches in length. The male is blue overall with a partially black face. Its wings have two prominent rust-colored wing bars. The female is a warm-buff color overall with two tan wing bars. Both sexes have the typical large beaks. Many people confuse this bird with the much smaller Indigo Bunting, which has no wing bars.

This bird is found over most of the southwest during the nesting season. However, the populations diminish in western Arizona, California, and northward. This bird has adapted to farmland where it prefers brushy areas and thickets near roadsides. In the arid areas of the southwest, brushy habitats near water are preferred.

The Blue Grosbeak prefers insects but will take seeds and berries. It usually feeds on or near the ground, hidden from view in the thickets. During non-breeding seasons, the Blue Grosbeak is found in a variety of habitats in small flocks. This summer resident migrates to central and South America for the winter.

The female Blue Grosbeak builds a well-constructed nest of twigs, roots, bark and weeds in thickets and shrubs. The nest is lined with finer material of grass and hair. Four or five light-blue eggs are incubated by the female for twelve days while the male attends her. The young leave the nest at ten days but the male will continue to feed them for a short time. The female may begin another brood.

Populations are increasing in the east and possibly in the west and southwest where the brushy habitats are present.

Top: **Blue Grosbeak**
Back: Female Front: Male

Bottom: **Black-headed Grosbeak**
Back: Female Front: Male

INDIGO BUNTING *Passerina cyanea*

The Indigo Bunting, at just over five inches long, is a common nesting bird in parts of the southwest. Most Indigo Buntings travel on to Mexico and Central America in April and May and again in August to October. The Indigo Bunting seems to be expanding its breeding range into the southwest since the 1950s.

The male Indigo Bunting has the typical conical finch bill and is deep-blue over its entire body. Its bill is gray. In low light, the males may appear completely black. The female is dull-brown overall and has a buff-colored breast with brown streaks. Her back has no discernible streaking. The wings and tail of the female have a hint of blue in them. Immature birds resemble the female.

The Indigo Bunting male sings from a high perch all summer long. The song is paired phrases, usually in twos, but occasionally in threes, given in a series. A common mnemonic is *fire fire where where here here put it out quick put it out quick.*

The Indigo Bunting's habitat is open weedy fields and grasslands with sporadic trees and tangle, woodland edges, park lands, railroad right-of-ways, and fence rows along fallow agricultural fields.

While the male Indigo Bunting is singing high up on his perch, the female is building the nest. Brambles, raspberry bushes, and thickets are the preferred nesting sites for this bird. It will also use small shrubs, trees, and even corn stalks. The female builds the nest alone from dried grasses, leaves, bark, Spanish moss, snake skins, and weeds. The oval-to-round nest is lined with rootlets, fine grass, plant down, and occasionally, feathers. The female incubates three to four blue-white eggs, often unmarked. She will incubate the eggs for two weeks or less. Both adults take care of the young until they fledge about twelve days later. The male takes a very active part in the foraging of food for the young. Like the Yellow Warbler, if the female finds the egg of a Cowbird she will cover it over with another nest, killing the cowbird eggs.

The Indigo Bunting is mostly a seed-eater but it does take berries and insects as well. In suburban backyards, the Indigo Bunting male will come to a thistle feeder for the first two to four weeks. To see the blue Indigo Bunting and the yellow American Goldfinch feeding at the same time is a feast for the eyes!

When immature males return to their nesting grounds and during migration, they may appear mottled and very scruffy as they are going through their molt. They will be bright-blue again in a few short weeks.

Indigo Bunting
Top: Female Bottom: Male

PAINTED BUNTING *Passerina ciris*

The Painted Bunting is one of the most colorful birds that breed in the southwest. A gap exists between the eastern and western populations. In the southwest, the Painted Bunting is found from Texas eastward and north into Oklahoma, Kansas, and Arkansas. In the southwest, it is a winter resident but is migratory, wintering in Mexico and Central America.

Wonderment is the common sentiment at the brilliant array of colors displayed by the Painted Bunting. At just over five inches long, the male Painted Bunting has a bright-blue head, lime-green back, dark wings and tail, and bright-red front and rump (top and bottom). It is almost as if this bird was put together by a committee. The female is a dull lime-green on the back and yellow-green on the front. The song of the Painted Bunting is a clear thin warble that is somewhat sing-songy and a bit drawn out.

The Painted Bunting prefers brushy and thickly-vegetated habitats along forest edges, railroad right-of-ways, fence lines, backyards, stream sides, and city and state parks. During migration, many people successfully attract this bird to their birdfeeding stations using birdseed. A popular place to find this bird at a feeder is Texas campgrounds and state parks.

During May, the female builds the nest in small trees and shrubs, occasionally in a tangle of ivy or vines. The nest is a deep cup, precisely made from grass, soft weeds, leaves, and ferns and lined with fine grasses and hair. Pale-brown spots concentrate around the large end of a pale gray-white, occasionally bluish, egg. Incubation by the female takes about twelve days. The male and female both tend the young. The young are fed partially-digested regurgitated seeds. As they near fledging they will be able to take whole seeds and some insects. The adults eat berries, fruits, and insects. In the south, two to three broods are common and four broods have been reported. In the northern part of its range one to two broods are normal.

In migration, the Painted Bunting can be seen in April through the first of June and again from late July through October. Each year there are reports of the Painted Bunting overwintering in central and southern Florida as well as possible breeding birds scattered throughout the state. Wherever they show up they cause excitement because of the combination of their bright colors.

Painted Bunting

VARIED BUNTING and LARK BUNTING

Passerina versicolor / Calamospiza melanocorys

Not as colorful as the Painted Bunting, the Varied Bunting is nevertheless a very pretty bird, especially in the bright sunlight. In the female plumage, this five-inch bird is a drab buff-gold with no accenting features. The male is quite different: its head is blue with a red nape, its body violet-purple, and its tail blue.

The Varied Bunting is a Mexican species that is found just across the border into Texas, in localized eastern and western parts of New Mexico, and into Arizona around Tuscon. Even in these limited areas it is here only during the breeding season.

The arid and semi-arid southwest is just right for the Varied Bunting's needs. Its habitat is along brushy stream sides and in canyons. It is easily seen when singing and can be approached quite closely. The Varied Bunting eats insects and seeds.

Its nest can be found three to five feet above the ground and is constructed of grasses and weeds and lined with soft fine materials. Four bluish-white eggs are incubated by the female for about two weeks. Both parents feed the young for about twelve days until they leave the nest. Two to three broods per year are produced.

Populations in the United States are stable. Some birds remain in the Big Bend National Park in Texas during the winter. Mexican populations may be declining because of local habitat changes.

The Lark Bunting male is easy to identify. It is black overall and about seven inches long with contrasting white wing patches which can be seen both in flight and at rest. The female is a heavily-streaked drab-brown. The female shows some white in her wings although not as pronounced as the male. Both sexes have pale-gray bills.

In the southwest, the Lark Bunting breeds in Texas, New Mexico, Oklahoma, Colorado, and Kansas. It is a winter resident along the Mexican border from California to central Texas. Occasionally these birds wander across the United States in fall migration. Populations appear to be stable but need to be monitored as prairie areas are depleted.

The Lark Bunting feeds extensively on insects during migration. After nesting, seeds are a greater portion of the food intake. During mating, the male does an aerial display, flying up into the air and fluttering about singing as he descends back to earth. The nest is placed on the ground but is well-hidden, sometimes in small holes. It is made from prairie grasses and lined with finer grasses, plant down, and hair. The four or five greenish-blue eggs are incubated by both sexes for about twelve days. The young grow very quickly with the rich prairie insect food and are able to leave the nest in about ten days. One brood each year is normal but in the southern range a second may occur.

Top: Varied Bunting
Back: Female Front: Male

Bottom: Lark Bunting
Back: Female Front: Male

RED-WINGED BLACKBIRD *Agelaius phoeniceus*

It has been said that the Red-winged Blackbird is the most numerous bird east of the Mississippi River. This is probably true because of the varying habitats in which the Redwing nests. In the southwest it is considered a permanent resident. The resident populations are increased during the winter with migrants from the north. The Red-winged Blackbird prefers marshes and shrubby wetlands but it has learned to adapt to old fields, forest edges, river valleys, parks, agricultural lands, and our suburban yards.

The male Red-winged Blackbird is aptly named, having a entirely black body with red epaulets, or patches, on the shoulders of his wings. The red is bordered by a narrow stripe of yellow. The male can control the amount of the epaulet it shows. When on display in defense of a female or territory, the red patch will be raised and showy. A large bird at about nine inches, the Red-winged Blackbird has a very pointed black bill used to catch insects, its main diet. The female is a dark streaked-brown above and lighter on the underside with heavy streaking. She has a tan cheek patch below a brown eye-stripe, above which is a tan eye-stripe. Immature males resemble the females but do evidence some of the red wing patches.

The nest is usually placed in dense marsh vegetation where it rises from the water. In brushy areas, it is placed in shrubs or dense herbaceous plants. The nest is made of grasses, sedges, rushes, and mosses intertwined with standing vegetation. The inner nest is lined with the same material except that it is finer.

In the marsh, the male Red-wing Blackbird has a harem of females in his territory. Each female builds her own nest and incubates the eggs for about twelve days. The eggs are pale-green with dark markings ranging from brown to purple. Four eggs are produced in each nest. Both adults feed the young a diet of insects for about two weeks at which time they are ready to leave. Being born over water for the most part, the young birds are able to swim in less than a week. In the southwest, nesting begins in April and two to three broods are produced.

In the winter huge flocks of northern migrants converge on the southwest and mix with the local populations. On occasion they may become a nuisance or be harmful to crops. The wintering birds eat more seeds and grain which makes it easy to attract this colorful bird to a birdfeeding station. Adult males leave the wintering grounds first, followed by adult females, then the immature birds. In the north, the return of the Red-wing Blackbird can be one of the first signs of spring.

Red-winged Blackbird
Right: Female   Left: Male

RUFOUS-SIDED TOWHEE   *Pipilo erythrophthalmus*

The Rufous-sided Towhee is a common year-round resident in the southwest. Its preferred habitat is forest edges, open woodlands, wooded parks, stream side thickets, and older wooded suburbs. In the southwest, the Rufous-sided Towhee is called the Spotted Towhee and both sexes have spots on the upper body which are absent in the eastern Towhee.

The male Rufous-sided Towhee has a black head, tail, and upper parts. Its tail has large white corners which are very showy in flight. His undersides are white and his flanks are "rufous"—a brick-orange color. He has a red eye. The female is an elegant chocolate-brown above which makes her quite beautiful in her own right, although not as striking as the male. In the southwest, the majority of these birds have white eyes instead of red, but the Rufous-sided Towhees found in the Texas Panhandle have varying shades of red eyes. During the winter, the red-eyed northern migrants merge with the resident populations.

The call of the Rufous-sided Towhee is *drink your teeee*, but a variety of other combinations are given. Upon arrival to the breeding ground in the spring, it seems as if they need a refresher course. The male may start for a day or so just doing the *drink* call and then, as if remembering, he will add the *your*. By the third or fourth day, he will add *teeeee*. Or he may skip a step and just call *drink teeeee*.

An identifying characteristic of the Rufous-sided Towhee is the way it feeds on the forest floor, where it scratches with both feet, raking back the leaves to expose seeds, grubs, and other invertebrates. The sound often seems to be much louder, as if a huge pile of leaves is being pushed away.

The Rufous-sided Towhee nests in small shrubs, palmettos, on the ground, or small thick trees. The female builds the nest out of twigs, grasses, weeds, bark strips, and leaves. The interior of the nest is lined with fine hair, grasses, and finely shredded bark. The female incubates the four gray to creamy-white eggs, marked with brown splotches on the larger end of the egg, for about thirteen days. Both sexes attend the young.

The young are fed predominately insects, but berries and fruit are added as they get older. In about twelve days the young are ready to fledge. Nesting begins in April and is usually complete by the end of the summer. In Florida up to three broods may be raised although two are more common. In the northern states only one brood is successful.

Rufous-sided Towhee
Top: Female Bottom: Male

GREEN-TAILED AND CANYON TOWHEE
Pipilo chlorurus / Pipilo fuscus

At six to seven inches in length, the Green-tailed Towhee is almost sparrow-like in appearance. It is more subtle in its coloration than the Rufous-sided Towhee. Its crown and nape are rust-red and its throat is white with black whisker marks accented with olive-green. Its call is a trill that begins with a *wheet chiirr* and ends with buzzy warbles. It also gives a cat-like *meow* like that of the Catbird.

The Green-tailed Towhee breeds in California, Nevada, Utah, and Colorado and winters in the southwest. In parts of Arizona, New Mexico, and Texas they are permanent residents. Its preferred habitats are open areas along rivers, in canyons, on mountainsides, or in brushy semi-arid areas. It feeds mainly on insects on the ground and seeds in season.

The male defends a territory by singing from a high perch and the female selects the mate. Its nest is placed on the ground or in a low shrub near the ground. The nest is usually quite large and made of twigs, grasses, and bark strips. The inner nest is finished with finer grasses, rootlets and hair. The four or five white eggs are spotted with brown and incubated for about two weeks. The young leave the nest in another two weeks.

The Canyon Towhee is a local bird in Arizona, southeastern Colorado, New Mexico, and Texas. In California, the Canyon Towhee is subdivided into the California Towhee.

The California Towhee is very similar to the Canyon Towhee, except it is plainer. To complicate matters, this bird was formerly called the Brown Towhee.

The eight-inch Canyon Towhee has a faint rust-red cap and nape. Its throat is buff-colored and outlined with dark spots. Its cheek is gray and streaked. Its overall body is a dull-gray brown, lighter underneath; its long tail is darker and rounded at the end.

The Canyon Towhee prefers the brushy and shrubby areas of the southwest. It can be found in relatively more arid dry canyons and moutainsides than the Green-tailed Towhee. It feeds on insects and seeds when available. It, too, feeds by scratching the ground with both feet but also by turning over leaves and sticks.

Nesting for life, the Canyon Towhee builds a bulky nest fairly low in a small shrub, tree, or cactus. It is constructed of twigs, weeds, and grasses and lined with finer leaves, grasses, plant down, and hair. The four or five eggs are whitish with mahogany spots. The female incubates the eggs for about eleven days and both parents attend the young for about twelve additional days until the young leave the nest. The young remain in the area begging for food for almost a week. Two to three broods are reared yearly. This bird seems to be stable in its populations but varies locally.

Top: Green-tailed Towhee
Bottom: Canyon Towhee

EASTERN AND WESTERN MEADOWLARK

Sturnella magna / Sturnella neglecta

The Eastern and Western Meadowlark are residents of the southwest and are common in areas where there are natural grasslands or fallow fields. The Western Meadowlark can be found over the entire southwest but the Eastern Meadowlark is only found to Arizona. These birds can be found in agricultural fields if the crops aren't harvested before nesting is complete. The Eastern Meadowlark can be found in many of the state parks and natural areas as well.

The Eastern Meadowlark is a fairly large stocky bird at over nine inches. Its breast is a bright-yellow and is set off by a broad black 'V' on its upper side. The sides of the Eastern Meadowlark are white with black streaks. Its back is brown with buff-colored feather edges, giving its back a scalloped look. Its head is somewhat flattened with a long pointed bill. The top of its head has tan and brown stripes from the bill to the back of the head. A little yellow shows in the eye-stripe forward of the eye. In flight, the white outer tail feathers are extremely noticeable.

When walking on the ground it flicks its tail, constantly showing the white feathers. This may be a mechanism to frighten insects or to confuse would-be predators. The only reliable way to tell these two bird apart is by their call: the Western Meadowlark has a beautiful flute-like call which is longer than the Eastern Meadowlark's more raspy call.

In the southwest, nesting begins in February.The male picks a dancing spot and stands erect with his bill pointed skyward. He dances around flicking his fanned-out tail. He flaps his wings and puffs out his bright-yellow breast feathers. The male often gets so excited he jumps up into the air and begins all over again. Upon acceptance the female joins the male but stays on the ground.

The nest is built by the female who makes a number of dummy nests before completing the final one. The nest is made entirely of heavy and light grasses and is domed with a side entrance. Occasionally fur and hair are used to line the inner nest.

The female lays four or five white eggs with brown or purple markings. She alone incubates the eggs for about two weeks. The male will help with the young which fledge in about twelve days. While a second nest is being built, the female will still be taking care of the young from the first nest. Two broods are normal in the southwest.

Winter brings an influx of birds into the southwest. Being predominately insect-eaters, the Meadowlarks find it hard going to remain in snow-covered areas. During the summer, the Meadowlarks eat grasshoppers, crickets, beetles, and a variety of larva. As fall and winter approach, a few seeds make up for the declining number of insects.

Eastern Meadowlark

GREAT-TAILED GRACKLE *Quiscalus mexicanus*

The Great-tailed Grackle is a large bird: the males are eighteen inches and the females are fifteen inches in length. They have an extremely long tail that fans out into a 'V' shape. The male has an iridescent purple head with bright-yellow eyes. Its body is a glossy black-purple.the female is dark-brown above and fawn below with a smaller tail. On the coast of Texas where the range of this bird overlaps with the Boat-tailed Grackle, the Great-tailed Grackle can be distinguished by its smaller size and yellow eyes.

In the southwest, the Great-tailed Grackle can be found from Texas north to Kansas and westward to California, New Mexico, and Arizona. It breeds in Colorado and Nevada. The Great-tailed Grackle sits on a pole or tree and makes a series of loud whistles followed by *kee kee kee kee* and *clack clack clack*. This bird is expanding its territory westward as well as northward and may soon become a permanent resident in areas in which it now only breeds.

The Great-tailed Grackle prefers open areas with mixed trees and shrubs. It prefers riparian habitats to arid areas. It has adapted well to suburbia and is found in city parks, farms, and older backyards. In its natural habitat it feeds it extensively on insects and seeds but in suburbia and around shopping centers it is totally opportunistic, taking whatever it can. It can be seen walking around the parking lots of fast food restaurants eating french fries, bits of hamburger, and donuts. In agricultural areas, it will follow farmers while they till the land.

Nesting occurs in small groups of fifteen to twenty-four pairs. Like the other grackles, it displays by spreading its wings and tail and raising its bill to the sky. A few males together will engage in a competition to see which one can point higher and better.

The nest is usually placed in trees between fifteen to forty feet above the ground, but it may be on a structure, cliff, or rarely, on the ground. The base nest is made of twigs, weeds, and grasses, and occasionally mud. The inner nest is lined with finer grasses and hair. Five or six brown-spotted greenish-gray eggs are incubated by the female for two weeks. Two additional weeks are needed for the young to fledge. Both parents attend the young. Two broods can be produced each year.

Great-tailed Grackle

HOODED ORIOLE *Icterus cucullatus*

This eight-inch Oriole is a summer resident of the southwest in the areas bordering Mexico and north into Arizona, Nevada, and California. This bird sometimes over-winters in parts of south-central Arizona. It prefers semi-arid to arid areas with water, such as by stream sides and in canyons. It seems to like palms and is expanding northward in California possibly because of landscaping patterns. It has adapted well to parks and stream side preserves where cottonwoods and sycamores are prevalent.

The male Hooded Oriole is a bright-orange to yellow-orange with black wings and tail. Its wings have one prominent wing bar and a faint second one. Its face and throat are also black with a black downcurved pointed bill. Immature males have the same pattern except their body is a green, similar to the females. The female Hooded Oriole is green-yellow and has the same patterns on her wings and tail, except she is just a bit darker (but not black), and she has no facial markings. The song is a series of whistles, deep trills, and squeaks.

The Hooded Oriole's diet is insects, nectar, and berries. During the spring when flowers are abundant, nectar and insects that attend the flowers make up a good part of its diet. In fact, spring is a good time to attract them to nectar feeders. However, as nesting begins they take nectar less frequently and feed more on insects for the protein needed by the young.

At the end of the season, they include berries in their diet.

The nest of the Hooded Oriole is not as deep as the 'sock' nests of some of the other orioles but is built the same manner. A forked branch, fairly high in a palm, yucca, cottonwood, or other deciduous tree is selected and a deep pendulous sack is woven. A wide variety of fibers are used to weave the nest: grasses, yarn, shredded bark, and Spanish moss. The interior of the pouch is lined with plant down, hair, and more Spanish moss. The female is the construction engineer with the male bringing the materials. The four or five blotched white eggs are incubated by the female for two weeks. Both parents attend the young for another two weeks until fledging. The young are quite noisy the last couple of days before fledging. Two broods are common, with a third in some seasons.

Populations in Texas have decreased because of Cowbird parasitism but seem to be recovering in some areas. The populations on the west coast seem to be expanding.

Hooded Oriole
Top: Female Bottom: Male

SCOTT'S ORIOLE *Icterus parisorum*

Scott's Oriole is different from most of the common orioles being a lemon color instead of the traditional orange-yellow. The nine-inch male is lemon-yellow overall with a black head, wings, and tail. The black on its head extends about half way down its back. Its wings have a pale wing bar and the top of its shoulder has a yellow spot. The female is also yellow but she has a gray head with a darker-streaked back. The gray on her head doesn't extend as far down as the male's. The call of Scott's Oriole is a series of deep full whistles.

In the southwest, Scott's Oriole is found in diverse habitats including thick oak forests, open fields with scattered shrubs and trees, semi-deserts, park land, and foothill canyons. Scott's Oriole feeds on tree caterpillars and, in the correct season, they eat nectar and berries. They have adapted to nectar feeders as well as fruit. Many times, when Scott's Oriole is feeding at flowers it takes not only but insects and flower parts as well.

In the breeding areas, the male sets up a territory by singing high in trees to entice the female. Once a female selects a male, they begin to build a nest in a yucca, Joshua tree, palm, or a deciduous tree. The nest, built by the female, is the typical bag although not as deep as some. It is woven from grasses, yucca fibers, yarn, and manmade fibers. The interior is lined with finer grasses, plant down, and hair. Three or four bluish eggs spotted with small dots of brown or gray are incubated by the female for two weeks. Both adults tend the young for another two weeks. Two broods are common during the year.

Scott's Oriole is found in Texas, New Mexico, Arizona, and Utah. Some local populations exist in California and have expanded from Utah into western Colorado. The Texas population is local near the Big Bend area. Populations seem to be stable to increasing. Some birds over-winter in southern Arizona.

Scott's Oriole
Back: Female Front: Male

ORCHARD ORIOLE *Icterus spurius*

The Orchard Oriole is a breeding resident of Texas, Oklahoma, Kansas, and eastern Colorado as well as a migrant on its way to South America for the winter or back to the United States to breed. A small population can be found in a local area of New Mexico.

In the southwest, the Orchard Oriole prefers open woodlands, forest edges, park lands, and suburban areas. Often this bird can be found feeding and nesting at stream sides where it forages along the edge. It is almost never found in a dense forest. The Orchard Oriole eats insects and occasionally berries. They can sometimes be enticed to take nectar from a feeder.

The male Orchard Oriole is a brick-red overall with a black head, tail, and wings. It has a faint buff-colored wing bar and its bill and legs are black. The female is olive-green above and greenish-yellow below. The wing of the female is a light-brown or olive-brown with two white wing bars.

The song of the Orchard Oriole resembles that of a Northern Oriole but is more rapid and varied. The song is a variety of loud whistles and chortles that seem to come from deep within the bird. The song is short with a drop at the end. A quick *wheer* at the end of the call can help in identification.

The nest of the Orchard Oriole resembles that of the Northern Oriole, although it is not as long and pendulous. Hung from the fork of a tree branch, it is usually between ten to fifty feet above the ground. The nest is woven with plant fibers including grasses, strings, Spanish moss, hair, and strips of fine bark. The cup is lined with fine downy material and grasses. The Orchard Oriole will hide its hanging nest by intertwining it with hanging leaves, small branches, or clumps of Spanish moss.

Markings on the eggs may be brown, purple, or any gradation between them. The overall color of the eggs is a light-blue to white. Four to five eggs are laid in the nest and are incubated by the female for nearly two weeks. The young birds are fed a heavy diet of insects and fledge in about two weeks. Both parents attend the young and many times they will remain together as a family group well into the fall. In certain parts of the United States these birds appear to nest in groups.

In the eastern United States, the population has had some problems due to habitat losses but in the southwest the populations are stable but increasing. Populations have increased to the north as well.

Orchard Oriole

Top: Female Bottom: Male

BLACK-THROATED SPARROW *Amphispiza bilineata*

The Black-throated Sparrow is a striking sparrow with a clear breast and large black throat. Its face is marked with white whiskers, a dark gray cheek, and white eye-stripe. Its crown, back, and rounded tail are dark-gray. The sexes are similar and are about six inches in length. The song is similar to the Song Sparrow's beginning with two quick clear notes and ending with a series of trills.

The Black-throated Sparrow is truly a bird of the southwest where it is found only from central Texas to California and northward to Nevada and Utah. A small local population exists in the panhandle of Oklahoma. It winters over in the states bordering Mexico. During the fall migration, it can occasionally be found in the midwest and on the east coast.

Arid brush lands are the preferred habitat for this little sparrow especially in the Sonoran Desert where they nest in creosote bushes and sagebrush flats. They also nest in open pinyon-juniper woods. The Black-throated Sparrow is versatile, taking what food it can as the opportunity arrives. In season, it feeds extensively on seeds and insects but also takes leaves, fruit, and buds from plants, especially to obtain water. Like the Song Sparrow, it runs around on the ground catching what it can, occasionally taking insects from shrubs and trees.

The rains bring on the nesting and mating season. The male sets up a territory and the female chooses her mate. Nests are hidden in shrubs and cacti a few feet from the ground. The bulk of the nest is composed of grasses, twigs, and weeds and is lined with fine grass, plant down and hair. Four pale eggs are laid and incubated for about fourteen days. The young are fed by both parents and two broods are usual.

In parts of the southwest, the Black-throated Sparrow has declined due to urban development. Unlike some other sparrows this bird has not yet adapted to suburban life. In the correct habitat it is fairly common and is holding its own.

Black-throated Sparrow

SONG SPARROW *Melospiza melodia*

The Song Sparrow is probably the most widespread of all the true sparrows. In the United States, it is found as a breeding bird over much of the northern states and well into Canada as far as Alaska. In Texas, New Mexico, Kansas, and Oklahoma, the Song Sparrow is a winter resident. It breeds in the remainder of the southwest. The highest concentration of breeding birds are found in the midwest.

The Song Sparrow ranges between five and seven inches with the male being the larger of the sexes. The overall color is brown but in the southwest it is a pale-brown while some California birds are quite dark. Its back, flanks, and breast are heavily streaked. Its breast shows a dark central spot. Its throat is light with pronounced whiskers or "malar" stripes. Its head is striped with brown and buff. Its tail is somewhat long, rounded at the end, and usually cocked to one side.

Hundreds of variations of its song have been recorded. Before going into a tirade of trills the Song Sparrow's call starts out with two or three clear whistles, occasionally four. One mnemonic for the call is *Marge Marge Marge take the kettle off the waters hot!* The call note is a sharp full note that sounds like *gail.*

The Song Sparrow's habitat is usually brushy open areas, thickets along stream sides, and woodland edges. Along the coast and in marshy areas, it can be found among thick herbaceous plants. In the winter, it is found wherever seeds can be found. It is very secretive, moving about on the ground and remaining hidden in the vegetation. In the summer, its food is largely insects but during the winter it eats seeds. Song Sparrows will readily come to birdfeeders in all seasons, especially if water is present.

The male sets up a territory early in the spring. He almost always sings from an elevated perch. The Song Sparrow's nest is usually well-hidden on the ground in a dense group of grasses. Occasionally, they nest above the ground in sturdy weeds or shrubs. The female builds an open cup-shaped nest of grasses and weeds. The nest is lined with hair, fine grass, and rootlets. The eggs are light-colored with heavy brown-spotted markings. Four or five eggs are incubated by the female for fourteen days. The young are able to leave the nest in about twelve days but will remain in the care of the parents for up to three weeks more. Two broods each year are common.

The Song Sparrow populations are stable and abundant. Where local habitats are being eliminated some local populations may be in jeopardy but overall the Song Sparrow is doing fine. During the winter, much of Canada is devoid of the Song Sparrow as they move to the southern parts of the continent.

Song Sparrow

LARK SPARROW *Chondestes grammacus*

The Lark Sparrow is a rather large striking sparrow at almost seven inches in length. Its head is a mixture of rufous red, white, and black stripes. Its throat is white with black whiskers bordered with white. Its cheek is rusty-red outlined in black and its crown and nape are alternating rufous and white stripes. Its back is a soft streaked brown and its breast gray-white with a bright central black spot. Its tail is long, rounded at the end with white tips and very noticeable in flight. Its song begins with a couple of clear notes followed by a series of musical and not so musical notes, interspersed with clear notes.

The Lark Sparrow breeds all over the southwest in the correct habitat. In California and Arizona, this sparrow can be absent in extreme desert situations. Its preferred habitat is open wood lots, riparian forests, brushy scrub land, oak savannah, and pinyon-juniper forests. During the winter, they can be found in more open areas and often are seen feeding in small flocks in grassy fields and agricultural areas. Feeding occurs while on the ground with insects making up the bulk of the diet in summer and more seeds during the winter.

The nest is built on the ground near some vegetation, possibly to hide the nest or shade it. Occasionally they will build in a shrub or tree up to about ten feet above the ground. The nest is constructed from grasses, twigs, and bark and is lined with fine bark fibers, rootlets, and fine grasses. After building the nest the female will incubate the five whitish brown-marked eggs for twelve days. The young are able to leave the nest in about six to ten days. Both parents attend the young. Two broods are common, especially in the south.

Populations in the east and midwest are declining due to habitat loss but the western and southwestern populations are stable. The highest nesting populations are in Texas north to Colorado and Kansas.

Lark Sparrow

AMERICAN AND LESSER GOLDFINCH
Carduelis tristis / Carduelis psaltria

The American Goldfinch, or 'wild canary,'breeds from well into Canada to just north of the southern tier of states. It winters south of this line over all of the southwest. Even though the Goldfinch is usually considered a permanent resident, the population does shift, usually in early fall.

The breeding plumage of the five-inch male is bright-yellow with a black cap, wings, and tail. The female is a drab olive-yellow and her wings and tail are not as dark. Faint wing bars are present. The male's winter plumage is similar to the female's with an overall olive color, drab wings and tail, and no head marking which makes it difficult to distinguish them apart in the winter. A telltale characteristic of this bird is the undulating flight with alternating flight and rests. Its song is a varied number of sweet twitters and tweets—the typical call being *perchickoree perchickoree.*

Its preferred habitats are open mixed areas, forest edges, and park land. It frequents weedy fields and roadsides where it can be seen perched on fences and tall weeds. Its favorite food is thistle and dandelion.

The American Goldfinch nests quite late in the summer. Its nest is a small compact cup and is built in the crotch of a deciduous tree about eight to fifteen feet above the ground. It is constructed of thistledown, spider webs, and soft plant fibers. It is so well constructed that it will even hold wa-

ter, sometimes drowning the unprotected chicks. The female incubates the five pale brown-spotted eggs for two weeks. Both sexes feed the chicks with regurgitated seeds and they leave the nest in about fifteen days. Their preferred feeder food is sunflower seeds and thistles (*niger*).

The Lesser Goldfinch breeds over California, Nevada, Utah, and Colorado and is a permanent resident south to the border. It is found eastward to southwestern Texas.

This small four-inch finch is yellow. The male has a yellow neck but its head, neck, back, and tail are black. The female looks like a small American Goldfinch but its undertail coverts are yellow. White wing bars are present with a white spot at the base of the primary feathers. The Lesser Goldfinch's song is similar to the American Goldfinch's.

The Lesser Goldfinch's preferred habitat is brushy stream sides, open country, and wood lots.It prefers seeds but will take insects.

Nesting occurs any time of the year in California and Arizona. Its nest is placed in the fork of a short tree or shrub. It is constructed of grasses, bark strips, and plant strips and lined with down and fine fibers. The five pale blue-green eggs are incubated by the female for twelve days. The male helps tend the young by regurgitating partially digested seeds. Two, possibly three, broods are raised each year.

Top two: American Goldfinch
Left: Female Right: Male

Bottom three: Lesser Goldfinch
Top: Black-backed Middle: Female
Bottom: Green-backed

247

HOUSE FINCH *Carpodacus mexicanus*

There are two separate populations of the House Finch. The eastern population started in the1980s with the release of some caged birds in New York and was very successfull. In the southwest, the five-inch House Finch can be found from Texas westward to the sea and northwestward to British Columbia.

The House Finch male is red with a brown cap, back, wings, and tail. Its breast is red above and streaked. Its belly is buff-colored and streaked. The male has a brown cheek. The female is a dull-brown overall, heavily streaked and lighter below. A variation that appears to be more prevalent in the southwest is that some males are lighter in color, being a pale yellow or orange.

Their preferred habitat in the southwest is semi-arid mixed forests, stream sides, chaparral, agricultural areas, and suburban and city situations. The only place it doesn't like is dense unbroken forests and open grasslands.

The House Finch eats almost any seeds, berries, or insects it can find, but it prefers seeds. In the summer, flowers, buds, and fruit make up a good part of its food. The adults feed their young partially digested seeds. It has readily adapted to birdfeeding stations. The food of preference is sunflower seeds; thistle is second. It has adapted to feeding from nectar feeders in the southwest and suet feeders in the north.

Nesting begins quite early in the year. Males sing most of the year and the female joins in in the spring. Its nest is built in trees, shrubs, or manmade structures such as shelves, wreaths, nest boxes, hanging baskets, or any flat structure. The female builds the base of the nest with weeds, twigs, and grasses. The inner nest is lined with finer material. The five eggs are pale-blue with dark dots clustered at one end. Two weeks are needed for the female to hatch the eggs and another for the parents to fledge the birds. The young follow the adults to feeders and beg for food. In the southwest, three broods are common and occasionally more.

House Finch
Back: Female Front: Male

VERDIN *Auriparus flaviceps*

This small four-inch bird is a true southwestern bird, usually found along the Mexican border and a small part of southern Nevada. It can also be found a couple hundred miles from the Mexican border from the southwest coast of Texas to the Pacific Ocean.

The Verdin is soft gray overall with a sunflower-yellow head and upper breast. Its gray body is accented by bright chestnut-colored shoulders. Its black eye and bill also accent its yellow head. Its song is a slow three-note whistle similar to the chickadee but the second note is lower. The call note is a rapid *chip*, almost a buzzing.

The Verdin is a bird of the arid and semi-arid southwest. It likes mesquite, desert valleys, and river sides and has adapted to subdivisions. In these areas it eats mainly insects. It feeds much like the Chickadee, looking under leaves and twigs, many times hanging upside down. It takes berries and seeds when available. It is possible to lure these birds to birdfeeding stations using nectar and water.

Nesting begins with the male building several nests from which the female selects one for incubation. The nest is built about chest-high in dense thorns, shrubs, or cacti. Its nest is quite large for such a small bird. The nest is in the shape of a ball and is made up of thorns, twigs, and weeds and lined with soft grasses, feathers, down, spiderwebs, and leaves. The entrance is in the lower half of the nest so water cannot get in, and is often placed on the side which catches the prevailing breezes in late season. The opposite is true at the beginning of the season when it is cooler; the entrance faces away from the prevailing breezes. The five eggs are a pale blue-green with reddish brown spots, often at the larger end. The female incubates the eggs for ten days and both parents feed the chicks for another three weeks.

Nests are well-constructed and are used during the winter for roosts. The young use the nest to sleep for a period of time after fledging. Populations seem to be holding their own, having adapted to backyard habitats.

Verdin

Index

Index